BLACK SABBATH
& OZZY OSBOURNE

THIS IS A CARLTON BOOK

Published by Carlton Books Ltd
20 Mortimer Street
London W1T 3JW

ISBN 978-1-78739-270-0

Editorial Director: Roland Hall
Project Editor: Ross Hamilton
Additional Editorial: Joel McIver
Design: Russell Knowles, James Pople
Production: Yael Steinitz
Picture Research: Steve Behan

A CIP catalogue for this book is available from the British Library

10 9 8 7 6 5 4 3 2 1

Printed in Dubai

BLACK SABBATH
& OZZY OSBOURNE

THE STORIES BEHIND
THE SONGS

CAROL CLERK & PAUL ELLIOTT

CARLTON
BOOKS

CONTENTS

IT WAS A SOUND
THAT SHOOK THE WORLD...

IN THE EARLY 1970S CAME THE FIRST GOLDEN AGE OF HEAVY METAL, DEFINED BY A HOLY TRINITY OF BRITISH BANDS: LED ZEPPELIN, DEEP PURPLE AND BLACK SABBATH. THE MUSIC WAS LOUD. IT WAS DECADENT. AND IT BLEW THE MINDS OF MILLIONS OF ROCK FANS.

The four members of Black Sabbath's original line-up – guitarist Tony Iommi, singer Ozzy Osbourne, bassist Geezer Butler and drummer Bill Ward – have never claimed that they invented heavy metal. By the time that Sabbath's debut album arrived in 1970, the wheels had already been set in motion by Zeppelin, Purple and, before them, Cream and Jimi Hendrix.

But with that first album, Black Sabbath took this form of music to a whole new level – to a different and darker place. Sabbath were the heaviest of the heavy.

The engine of the Sabbath sound was Iommi's grinding riffing, and the anguished wailing of Osbourne was a voice that had never been heard before. With songs that spoke of horrors both real and imagined – Satan, war, psychosis – Black Sabbath reigned supreme as the scariest rock band on God's Earth. And that sound, with its elemental power, would have a profound influence over generations of metal bands.

The founding members of Black Sabbath were genuine working class heroes, raised in Britain's second largest city, Birmingham. The success of landmark albums such as *Paranoid* and *Sabbath Bloody Sabbath* made them million-selling superstars. A decade of drug-fuelled excess led inevitably to an implosion, and in 1979 Osbourne was fired from the band. But the last album that Sabbath made with Ozzy in the 70s had a title that would prove prophetic: *Never Say Die!*.

Ozzy had his revenge when he became a huge solo star in the 80s. Adding to his fame was his reputation for lunacy. He was the man who bit the head off a bat and pissed on a sacred American monument, The Alamo

Cenotaph. In his absence, Sabbath continued for 18 years, with mixed fortunes. In all that time, Tony Iommi was the sole constant – the keeper of the flame. Many band members came and went, most prominent among them Ronnie James Dio, the singer who had replaced Ozzy in 1980.

And yet, for Ozzy, Sabbath always felt like unfinished business. In 1997, the original Black Sabbath reunited. They toured, on and off, until 2005, when Ozzy resumed his solo career and Iommi and Butler teamed up once more with Ronnie James Dio as Heaven & Hell. But in the wake of Dio's death in 2010, it was decided that Ozzy would again return to Black Sabbath – this time, to make a new album.

It was no easy task. Iommi was battling cancer, and Bill Ward resigned in a contractual dispute. Nevertheless, the album was completed with Rage Against The Machine drummer Brad Wilk. It was released in 2013 with the simple title of *13*. And it proved that Black Sabbath – described by the album's producer Rick Rubin as "the forefathers of heavy metal" – were still the masters of the art. A final tour, dubbed The End, proved this one last time.

Ozzy said that with this album, his life had turned full circle. And so too had the story of Black Sabbath, the greatest and most influential heavy metal band of them all...

Above: The final, triumphant line-up of Black Sabbath in action; although Ozzy Osbourne, Tony Iommi and Geezer Butler participated, Bill Ward stayed away.

Opposite: The Prince of Darkness himself, Ozzy. It's been a long and spectacular ride for the Aston kid born John Osbourne.

THE EARLY YEARS

IN THE LATE 60S, FOUR YOUNG MUSICIANS FROM BIRMINGHAM
QUIT THEIR RESPECTIVE BANDS TO JOIN FORCES IN A NEW GROUP.
THEY STARTED OUT PLAYING BLUES, BUT ONE SONG THEY WROTE
TOGETHER WOULD CHANGE EVERYTHING. IT WOULD GIVE THIS GROUP
A NEW NAME AND A NEW SOUND: BLACK SABBATH WAS BORN.

Ozzy Osbourne once said of the creation of Black Sabbath: "It was like it was destined to happen."

He explained: "Black Sabbath was four guys born and raised within a few miles of each other. I was in school with Tony. Geezer was in my first band. We were just local boys made good."

It all sounds so simple. In reality, it was anything but.

It was in the early 60s that Ozzy first met Tony Iommi, when they attended the same school in Birmingham – Birchfield Road Secondary Modern in the city's Perry Barr district. "Tony was a year older," Ozzy recalled. "He could look after himself – he could fight. Everybody knew that. So I stayed out of his way."

It was just as well. In those days, Iommi held no affection for Ozzy. As he told *Q* magazine: "We were in different gangs. I didn't like him."

At a distance, Ozzy remained in awe of Iommi's ability as a guitar player. "I remember him coming to school with a red guitar and playing Shadows songs," he said. "I didn't know anyone our age who could play music."

But in 1965, shortly after he had left school, Iommi suffered a horrific injury that left him fearing he would never play the guitar again. Working at a sheet metal factory, his right hand was trapped in a guillotine press, and the tips of the two middle fingers were chopped off.

At 17, Iommi thought that his dream of a career in rock and roll was over. What lifted him out of his depression was a gift from the factory manager – a record by Django Reinhardt, the Belgian-born jazz guitarist who attained legendary status despite having lost the use of two fingers to paralysis caused by a fire.

Necessity being the mother of invention, Iommi fashioned two "thimbles" for his fingertips by melting down a plastic washing-up liquid bottle to form two pieces that he capped with leather from an old jacket. Then, like Django, he learned again how to play: a left-handed guitarist, he developed a new fretting style using primarily the two remaining "good" fingers. As a result, he would find a sound that was uniquely his own.

By 1968, at the height of the British blues-rock boom, Iommi was playing with Mythology, a band based in Carlisle and billed somewhat extravagantly as "Cumberland's answer to the Jimi Hendrix Experience." The band's drummer was Bill Ward. But Iommi was looking for a better opportunity. So too was Ozzy, who was then fronting Rare Breed, for which Geezer Butler was playing rhythm guitar.

Ozzy and Iommi would cross paths, four years after they had last seen each other, when Ozzy quit Rare Breed and advertised his services in a local newspaper.

"I gave myself a grand stage name," Ozzy recalled, laughing. The ad read: 'Ozzy Zig needs a gig.' There was a contact address at 14 Lodge Road, the Osbourne family home. And within a few days came a knock

at the door. "I saw this big blue van parked outside," Ozzy said. "My dad thought it was the cops. Then I saw Tony sitting in the front of the van."

When Iommi recognized 'Ozzy Zig' from his school days, he was less than happy. "I read his lips," Ozzy recollected. "He said, 'Fucking hell, not him – he's a cunt.' He nearly drove off."

Instead, Iommi decided to give Ozzy a chance. It was one of the smartest decisions he ever made.

Iommi and Osbourne formed a new group with Ward on drums and Butler switching to bass. Named the Polka Tulk Blues Band, they were briefly a six-piece, with a second guitarist and a saxophone player – both of whom were ousted when the band was renamed Earth. Their music was simple. "We were a blues band," Iommi said.

In December '68, Earth might have folded when Iommi was poached by folk-rock band Jethro Tull to replace guitarist Mick Abrahams. Iommi appeared with Tull in *The Rolling Stones Rock And Roll Circus*, an all-star concert filmed for the BBC. But he quickly fell out with Tull leader Ian Anderson. Iommi was his own man. And when Earth regrouped, he had a new agenda.

Inspired by the first Led Zeppelin album, Iommi vowed to make music that was, in his words, "even heavier". And in the spring of 1969, the band wrote the song that would shape their entire career.

It was based around a monolithic three-note riff that had a dark and sinister feel. In the lyrics were visions of Satan and hellfire. And in a stroke of genius, they named this song after a 1963 horror movie starring Boris Karloff: *Black Sabbath*.

On August 26, 1969, at Banklands Youth Club in the northeastern town of Workington, the band played for the final time as Earth. From that point on, they would be known as Black Sabbath.

The new name was not to everyone's liking. "Alvin Lee from Ten Years After was a good friend of ours," Ozzy said. "When we told him

we were calling the band Black Sabbath, he said, 'I don't like it. You won't get anywhere calling yourselves that.'"

He could not have been more wrong. By the end of that year, the band had recorded their debut album, and after rejections from 14 record companies, they signed to Philips.

A new decade was about to begin, a new era for rock music. Black Sabbath's time had come.

Opposite: Yes, that is a young Ozzy Osbourne performing naked in 1969, but as for who the rest of the band are, consult the internet for several interesting theories.

Above, top: Ozzy and Tony pictured in their early days together. Their roles were already established, with the singer a madman and the guitarist a (relatively) restrained virtuoso.

Above: Poster for the 1963 horror movie *Black Sabbath*. The band took the film's title for their first song – and, later, for the name of the band.

THE 1970S

IT WAS THE DECADE IN WHICH BLACK SABBATH ROSE FROM
OBSCURITY TO BECOME ONE OF THE BIGGEST BANDS IN THE WORLD.
THEY SOLD MILLIONS OF ALBUMS AND LIVED THE ROCK AND ROLL
LIFESTYLE TO EXCESS. BUT AT THE END OF THE 70S, THE BAND
WAS IN DISARRAY AND FACING AN UNCERTAIN FUTURE.

For Black Sabbath, success came quickly – and on a scale that Ozzy described, with characteristic bluntness, as "fucking unbelievable."

In March 1970, the band's debut album, titled simply *Black Sabbath*, hit Number 8 on the UK chart. "My knees went to jelly," Ozzy recalled to *Q* writer Phil Sutcliffe. "From that moment, my life went off like a rocket."

Before the year was out, Sabbath had a huge hit single with 'Paranoid'. The album of the same name hit Number 1. And fresh from this success, the band embarked on their first US tour.

This would prove a revelatory experience. "It was on that trip that we first discovered pot," Ozzy said. But no amount of dope smoking was going to soften Black Sabbath. The hippie idealism of the 60s meant nothing to four men who had known only the grim reality of post-war Birmingham. As Ozzy said: "That 'go to San Francisco with a flower in your hair' thing... You might as well have said, 'Go to Mars'." Black Sabbath came from a place where life was hard, and there was a sense of this in their music.

From 1970 through to 1975, Black Sabbath were unstoppable. In this period they made six classic, genre-defining albums: *Black Sabbath, Paranoid, Master Of Reality, Vol. 4, Sabbath Bloody Sabbath* and *Sabotage*. All reached the Top 10 in the UK. Four made the US Top 20.

Sabbath also toured relentlessly, and played to vast audiences. A quarter of a million people saw them perform at the California Jam festival on April 6, 1974, an event co-headlined by Deep Purple and Emerson, Lake & Palmer. As Bill Ward recollected to *Classic Rock*: "We were flying high, high, high..."

But the good times couldn't last forever. By 1976, a growing sense of disillusionment and ennui had begun to eat away at the four members of Black Sabbath. The years spent on the road and the madness that went with it – the booze, the drugs, the women – was taking its toll. And although the band had sold millions of records, a protracted legal battle with their former manager had cost them dear. "Most of our money went on lawyers and taxes," Geezer Butler said.

Sabbath's problems were compounded when their 1976 album *Technical Ecstasy* underperformed. For the first time, a Sabbath album failed to make the UK Top 10. Worse, it didn't even make the Top 50 in

"WE WERE NAÏVE...WE CERTAINLY DIDN'T KNOW ANYTHING ABOUT THE OCCULT."

Ozzy Osbourne

America. And it was at this point that Ozzy Osbourne started to become restless. As he later revealed: "I lost interest after *Technical Ecstasy*." In 1977, he quit the band. "I wanted to do something different," he said. "I wanted to do a solo album."

Tony Iommi had no idea if Ozzy was gone for good. But he was certain that this would not be the end of Black Sabbath. He contacted a singer named Dave Walker, who had been a member of blues-rock outfit Savoy Brown, and also Fleetwood Mac. Walker joined Sabbath for rehearsals. They wrote some songs together. And on January 6, 1978, the new-look Black Sabbath appeared on the BBC Midlands TV show *Look! Hear!*. They performed their classic track 'War Pigs', and a formative version of a new song, 'Junior's Eyes'.

Then, Ozzy had a change of heart, and Dave Walker was out. On January 28, it was announced that Ozzy had rejoined Black Sabbath. With a studio in Toronto already booked in advance, a new album was recorded in February. And in May, the band celebrated their tenth anniversary with a UK tour. But if that tour was intended as a victory lap, it did not play out that way.

Opposite: Is there anything more Seventies than Ozzy in silver boots and Tony in a sky-blue cape? It's possible that drugs were ingested before (and after) this photo was taken

Above: The Sab Four: from left, Ozzy Osbourne, Geezer Butler, Tony Iommi and Bill Ward. Alongside Led Zeppelin and Deep Purple, they pioneered heavy metal.

We were fucked up on drugs," Ozzy said. And in this state, Sabbath were no match for their support act. Van Halen, from California, were the new heroes of American rock. They had in Edward Van Halen the most exciting rock guitarist since Hendrix; and in David Lee Roth, a blond Adonis of a frontman who made Ozzy look like a fat old has-been.

In 1970, Sabbath had represented the future of rock. Eight years on, Van Halen were the future, and Sabbath had become yesterday's men.

Never Say Die! – the album recorded in Toronto – fared no better than *Technical Ecstasy*, even if the title track was a hit in the UK. And on the US tour that followed, Ozzy's drinking and drug taking was spiraling out of control. The others were no saints, but as Iommi said: "Ozzy was on a different level."

For Black Sabbath and Ozzy Osbourne, the writing was on the wall…

Opposite: Hot in the shade(s): Ozzy may have been California dreaming, but his English roots never deserted him – hence the immortal V-sign.

Right: Venusians in furs: Tony and Ozzy wowing America, and reaping the rewards of that seminal series of early Sabbath albums.

Below: The leather years: before the crazy clothes colours kicked in, black was the only way to go for Sabbath (because that was all they could afford)..

BLACK SABBATH
(1970)

IT WAS RECORDED IN A MATTER OF HOURS, AND YET ITS IMPACT
WOULD ECHO THROUGH THE DECADES. THE FIRST BLACK SABBATH
ALBUM IS ONE OF THE SEMINAL ROCK RECORDS, A TOUCHSTONE
FOR COUNTLESS HEAVY METAL BANDS. AND AS METALLICA'S JAMES
HETFIELD CONFESSED: "IT SCARED THE SHIT OUT OF ME."

Black Sabbath didn't know they were playing the Devil's music. It just sort of happened.

In early 1969, when Tony Iommi wrote the riff for the song that would be named 'Black Sabbath', he knew immediately that he was on to something. He had been listening to *The Planets* by English composer Gustav Holst – in particular, the first movement, 'Mars, The Bringer Of War'. Playing variations on this theme, Iommi developed a three-note motif that had a strange kind of resonance. It sounded not simply heavy, but eerily dark.

It was a sound that made the hairs on Iommi's arms stand up. And when Bill Ward first heard this riff, he was struck by what he called "a power that I found totally compelling."

Serendipity played a part in the creation of this song. Opposite the building in Birmingham where the band rehearsed was a cinema. On one evening, Geezer Butler had watched as people queued for a screening of a horror film by Italian director Mario Bava, originally titled *I Tre Volti Della Paura* (*The Three Faces of Fear*) and named for its British release as *Black Sabbath*. "It was strange," Butler observed, "that people spend so much money to see scary movies."

From this came the band's modus operandi: to make scary music. They took the film's title for their powerful new song – and later, for the name of the band. And to fit the heavy vibes of Iommi's riff – what Ward referred to as "dark notes" – Ward and Ozzy wrote lyrics in which Satan appeared to claim another soul.

"We were naïve," Ozzy admitted many years later. "We certainly didn't know anything about the occult." And yet Iommi, in his naivety, had replicated in those three notes a harmonic scale known for centuries as *Diabolus in musica* – the Devil in music.

This dissonant scale was first identified in the Middle Ages and achieved such a visceral effect of impending doom that it was banned in God-fearing European society. Most infamously, it was featured in Italian composer Giuseppe Tartini's *Devil's Trill Sonata* in the eighteenth century, a work the composer claimed was written after Satan visited him in a dream.

Tony Iommi knew nothing of this. All he was trying to do was make music that was heavier than Led Zeppelin. Unwittingly, he had created what was, in the words of Judas Priest singer Rob Halford, "the most evil song ever written."

According to Ozzy, Sabbath's debut album was recorded in one session, "12 hours straight". Tony Iommi remembers it differently: three afternoons on consecutive days. What is certain is that Sabbath's debut album was made quickly because it had to be. Without a record deal in place, the band's manager Jim Simpson borrowed what he could from Essex Music, the publishing company to which Sabbath were signed. Simpson got £500. It was enough.

The recording took place with producer Rodger Bain in October 1969 at Regent Sound studio in London's Denmark Street. And as Ozzy explained: "Really, that album was the live show without the audience. We'd been doing the songs live on stage for over a year or so. We didn't have to sit down and think about what we were gonna do. We just played it."

For much of the album they played super-heavy, on riff-driven songs such as 'The Wizard', 'Behind The Wall Of Sleep' and 'N.I.B.'. The latter featured more devilry – Ozzy as the voice of Lucifer – although its title, often misinterpreted as an acronym for Nativity In Black, was in fact an in-joke about Bill Ward's beard being shaped like the nib of an ink pen.

In addition, there were two tracks on which Sabbath exhibited a broader stylistic range. Both were cover versions. 'Evil Woman' – essentially a pop song – was originally recorded by little-known Minnesota band Crow. "The record company insisted that we did that

Opposite: A Rock! flyer presenting forthcoming events at the Liverpool Stadium in 1970. Black Sabbath were supported by progressive rock bands Yes and East of Eden.

ROCK!

TRIAD PRESENTS AT THE LIVERPOOL STADIUM .

NEWSLETTER NO I

TWO THOUSAND SIX HUNDRED PEOPLE CAME TO SEE FREE,MOTT THE HOOPLE,TREES,
AND BRONCO ON SAT SEPT I9TH AT THE STADIUM.POSSIBLY A LOT MORE WOULD
HAVE TURNED UP IF SOMEONE HADN'T STARTED A RUMOUR THAT THE CONCERT WAS
SOLD OUT A WEEK IN ADVANCE.TICKETS,WHICH COST I4/- WERE CHANGING HANDS FOR
A POUND IN LOCAL SCHOOLS WHICH WAS RIDICULOUS AS WE ARE REALLY TRYING TO
KEEP PRICES DOWN.DON'T BE FOOLED - RING THE STADIUM 051-236-6316.

COMING

SATURDAY NIGHTS   USUALLY 7.p.m. - II.45 p.m.

IOTH OCT   CAT STEVENS - QUINTESSENCE - AMAZING BLONDEL - GREASY BEAR -
           MEDICINE HEAD.TICKETS I2/- IN ADV I4/- At DOOR

7TH NOV   TYRRANOSAURUS REX - MATTHEWS SOUTHERN COMFORT - PRETTY THINGS -
           SAM APPLE PIE   IN ADV I2/6 ATV DOOR I5/-

28TH NOV   EDGAR BROUGHTON - FORMERLY FAT HARRY - THIRD EAR BAND - KEVIN
           AYERS AND THE WHOLE WORLD - MICHAEL CHAPMAN AND HIS BAND. IN ADV
           IO/- AT DOOR I2/6.

5TH DEC   BLACK SABBATH - YES - EAST OF EDEN - STRAY TICKETS I2/6 - I5/-DOOR

TRAFFIC ARE BOOKED FOR THE NEW YEAR - MOTT THE HOOPLE AFTER THEIR INCREDIBLE
PERFORMANCE ON THE I9TH WILL BE BACK AS SOON AS POSSIBLE - THE DOORS ARE
UNDER DISCUSSION FOR MARCH AND THERE IS A POSSIBILITY OF JONI MITCHELL
DOING A CONCERT FOR US SOMETIME NEXT YEAR.AS SOON AS JOE COCKER HAS A GROUP
WE'VE GOT A JOE COCKER CONCERT......WE SINCERELY ADVISE YOU TO BUY TICKETS
IN ADVANCE - IT'S CHEAPER - YOU GET IN HALF AN HOUR EARLIER,AND WE WORRY
LESS...TICKETS FROM RUSHWORTH AND DREAPER,WHITECHAPEL LIVERPOOL,ON THE
EIGHTH DAY I9 NEW BROWN ST MANCHESTER,W.A.GUY 75 FOREGATE CHESTER,DAWSON'S,
65 SANKEY ST. WARRINGTON.TICKETS BY POST - SEND A P.O. AND S.A.E. TO
THEATRE BOOKINGS,RUSHWORTH AND DREAPER,WHITECHAPEL,LIVERPOOL.TEL 051-709-8070
YOUR DJ IS ANDY DUNKLEY WITH SIMON FOSTER ASSISTING.
MAGAZINES BY MIKE DON FOOD BY THE FAR OUT FOOD FARM (OR SOMETHING)

IF YOU WANT TO SEE ANY GROUPS WE HAVEN'T BOOKED YET DROP US A LINE AT THE
STADIUM,ST PAUL'S SQ. LIVERPOOL.THE STADIUM IS RIGHT NEXT TO EXCHANGE STATION

song," Ozzy grumbled. It was released as Sabbath's debut single in January 1970, and flopped. There was also evidence of the band's blues roots in their version of 'Warning', a 1967 single by The Aynsley Dunbar Retaliation, transformed by Sabbath into a trippy 10-minute jam.

But what defined this album was that one "evil" song. It was the opening track, prefaced by a chillingly atmospheric introduction: the sound of rainfall, rumbling thunder and the ominous tolling of a church bell. It had a raw power greater than anything that had come before it. For many, this was the first true heavy metal song. And the Satanic imagery sealed the band's reputation: Black Sabbath, the Devil's disciples. "It was great to have that kind of image," Geezer Butler said. "Because people were going, 'Well, are they or aren't they?'"

The album was released in February 1970 – on Friday the 13th, of all days. In its original vinyl format it had a gatefold sleeve, which opened to reveal an inverted crucifix.

Reviews were mostly bad. America's *Rolling Stone* magazine mocked Sabbath's music and occult imagery, describing the album as "like Vanilla Fudge playing doggerel tribute to Aleister Crowley." It didn't matter. In the UK, the album made the Top 10. In the US, it would sell a million copies.

Black Sabbath had arrived.

Above: Bill delivers the jazz-influenced vibes, the other three headbang politely. Did America "get" Black Sabbath immediately? No indeed, and you can see why.

Opposite: A Midnight Concert flyer signed by the four founding members of Black Sabbath (Tony Iommi, Bill Ward, Geezer Butler and Ozzy Osbourne). Barclay James Harvest and Quatermass performed at the event.

"WE DIDN'T HAVE TO SIT DOWN AND THINK ABOUT WHAT WE WERE GONNA DO. WE JUST PLAYED IT."

Ozzy Osbourne

BLACK SABBATH

The doom-laden title track of the band's first album has become one of the great rock classics of all time. From beginning to end, from the eerie, opening sounds of a rainstorm and a church bell through the monstrous riffs and sinister melodies that lead to a climactic guitar solo, this is classic Sabbath.

The genuinely disturbing music is matched by a set of lyrics about a smirking Satan who is chasing his "chosen one" – the song's narrator – as the flames of hell burn ever higher and the victim flees, with Ozzy wailing, "Oh, no!" and pleading, "Please God, help me!"

It's a scenario which should logically have been interpreted as a fantasy that, if anything, clearly warned against any forays into the black arts, but this was overlooked by listeners who preferred to link the track and the very mention of the word Satan to the overwhelming body of evidence – the aluminium crosses, the album sleeve, the musical force – that had already placed Ozzy, Iommi, Butler and Ward on the dark side of the spiritual fence.

The track pre-dated the band's change of name to Black Sabbath, erupting spontaneously in a humble four-track studio in London's Tottenham Court Road, where they were recording demos. Ozzy recalled a simple sequence of events: "We started writing heavy riffs, wrote the song 'Black Sabbath' and then we changed our name."

"'Black Sabbath' was written on bass," Geezer Butler recalled in *Bass Frontiers* magazine. "I just went into the studio and went, 'Bah, bah, bah,' and everybody joined in and we just did it. However long the song is was how long it took us to write it. Like 'NIB' just started with me doing the bass riff and everybody joined in. In those days, we didn't have tape recorders or anything, and nobody would write stuff at home and bring it to the studio. We just used to jam for two or three hours and see what came out."

Ozzy would spontaneously weigh in with melody lines and the odd lyric and Iommi, well, he was the man who most often sparked the songs, just messing around on the guitar. He was, according to Ozzy, "the master of fucking riffs."

Even more generously, the singer adds: "We never realized at the time how fucking clever he was." With each song worked out on the spot, Geezer Butler would later add vocals.

While Geezer sees 'Black Sabbath' as a bass-driven creation, Iommi vividly remembers it springing to life from a guitar riff that simply came to him, and Ward – who drummed with his body, heart, soul and massive cymbals – cites the track as a particularly good example of his tom-tom work and swing rhythms.

But every member of the band agrees that 'Black Sabbath' – like the other album tracks – happened almost by itself; they never had to wait for the elusive muse. Bill Ward, for one, believes they were being guided…

THE WIZARD

Tony Iommi enjoyed Geezer's interest in the supernatural: he was delighted that it separated the group from their contemporaries, and it particularly suited his enormous, gates-of-hell guitar riffing.

But the abrasive motif he contributed to "The Wizard" was perhaps out of step with the lyrics, which are rightly regarded as an embarrassment – they are too cheery, too primary school.

Dressed with harmonica, the song talks of evil powers and demons – all well and good except that these forces from the underworld come over all worried and "magically disappear" when the wizard strolls through the neighbourhood wearing fancy clothes, ringing a bell and casting a benevolent spell or two. The possibility exists that the wizard might be intended as a characterization of God and the song as a cynical comment on worshippers' blind faith, although this is not specified in the lyric.

Whatever, the respectable citizens in the song are relieved to be rid of the fiendish demons – they all "give a happy sigh", which isn't exactly what you might expect from Black Sabbath, two tracks into their controversial first album.

Ozzy, however, still defends the imagery: "If a wizard walked up to you, you'd definitely go, 'Fuck me, there's a wizard!'" The track would later turn up as the B-side for the band's future hit single, "Paranoid".

NIB

The meaning of the title has long been debated, with many fans believing that it stands for "Nativity In Black". But according to Ozzy, it represents something much less mysterious.

He explained: "We were all stoned in Hamburg and Bill used to have this really long, pointy beard and I said, 'Hey Bill, you look like a pen nib.' So when Geezer said, 'What are we going to call this song?' I said, 'Oh, call it NIB.'"

The title, therefore, is completely unconnected to the track, which is lyrically fanciful, imagining a scenario in which the Beast himself has fallen in love – "Look into my eyes, you'll see who I am/My name is Lucifer, please take my hand."

"There's only two songs that even mention Satan or Lucifer on the first album," said Geezer Butler in a 1997 interview. "The song "Black Sabbath"… and "NIB" is a tongue-in-cheek thing about how Lucifer would feel about everything if he fell in love with someone, which I thought was a reasonably humorous thing to write about.

"But, of course, people in America just picked up on the words Satan and Lucifer, didn't listen to any of the other lyrics and condemned us. Which is sad, because some of my other Black Sabbath lyrics – "After Forever" (from 1971's *Master Of Reality*) as an example – are as religious as anything you'll ever read."

Returning to the topic of black magic, Ozzy sighed: "No matter how much you'd tell these people it's not for real, they'd go, 'Oh yeah, but we know,' and wink. Even "NIB" on our first album was a humorous song about the Devil falling in love, and I thought it was hysterical. But nobody got the point…"

EVIL WOMAN (DON'T PLAY YOUR GAMES WITH ME)

Black Sabbath's first single, backed with "Wicked World", was released twice within three months – first by Fontana in January 1970 and again in March when the group moved to the Vertigo label.

"Evil Woman", slightly more commercial than the rest of the album tracks, was a cover of a song by a Minnesota band called Crow and another of the cuts emerging from the Regent Sound sessions in Tottenham Court Road.

The single flopped both times, but Ozzy was unconcerned. It was enough for him that he had made a record to take home and show

his mother. It didn't occur to him, or to his fellow bandmates, that the original material they were irrepressibly coming up with would become their passport to untold wealth and infamy.

But they did realize that they had hit on something different and extremely powerful, almost without trying. Bill Ward is reluctant to take any of the credit for this. In an extraordinary interview with author Steven Rosen, he talked of the spooky coincidences that occurred during the band's early years, with all four members, on one occasion, reporting the same dream. He also proposed that there was a fifth, invisible member of Black Sabbath.

"The fifth member of Black Sabbath was whatever the phenomenon was," he told Rosen in all seriousness. "A lot of the times we didn't write the fucking songs at all. We showed up and something else wrote them for us. We were conduits."

Ward revealed that Ozzy's father, Jack, was aware of some strangeness around the band, recognizing that, "there was something going on here that possibly he couldn't understand, but he knew it was real…" Jack also knew that, "there'd been some kind of phenomenon going on here that nobody was quite sure of."

Ozzy is less dramatic about his father's reactions to Black Sabbath, recently saying: "I remember when the first album came out I thought, 'Great, I can show my dad.' We put it on the old radiogram and I remember him looking at Mum with this really confused look on his face and turning to me and saying, 'Son, are you sure you're just drinking the occasional beer?'"

Other tracks on the album are 'Behind The Wall Of Sleep' ("I always thought that your dreams were telling you what death was going to be like, after a particularly weird dream I had," said Geezer) and the four-line poem that is 'Sleeping Village', an unsettling, acoustic snippet segueing into the blues-influenced 'Warning', which laments a lost love and includes a long guitar solo. It was longer still, around 18 minutes, before being cut in the mix, much to Iommi's disappointment.

Above: Black Sabbath's early albums were recorded in a matter of days… and this famous studio shot reveals why. The studio had very little in the way of entertainment.

Next spread: The band take part in an outdoor photo shoot… along with a profoundly uninterested bystander.

PARANOID

(1970)

JUST FOUR MONTHS AFTER THE RELEASE OF THEIR DEBUT ALBUM, BLACK SABBATH RETURNED TO THE SAME STUDIO TO RECORD THE FOLLOW-UP. AMONG THE POWERFUL NEW SONGS THEY HAD WRITTEN WAS 'WAR PIGS'. BUT IT WAS A SONG THEY KNOCKED TOGETHER AT THE LAST MINUTE THAT WOULD MAKE THIS THE MOST FAMOUS ALBUM OF SABBATH'S CAREER.

In June 1970, Black Sabbath were back at Regent Sound studios to cut their second album. They retained the services of producer Rodger Bain. And again, they made fast work of it. The whole album was completed within a few days – four at most, according to Tony Iommi – with some additional recording done at another London studio, Island.

Several songs for the album, including 'War Pigs', had been written while the band was on tour. Others had come together during a week of rehearsals in Monmouth in Wales. And one song was created on the spot, in the studio, on the final day of recording. Written in just 20 minutes and recorded within an hour, it would become the title track of the album and a major hit single.

Famously, this song was written only because Rodger Bain insisted that the album needed another track. The band felt that they already had enough. Luckily for them, the producer pushed them for something more.

Iommi wrote the speedy, fuzz-toned riff alone, while the others were on a lunch break. Geezer Butler already had a rough draft of lyrics and the title. And once Ozzy had worked out a vocal melody, it was done.

'Paranoid' distilled the essence of Black Sabbath into 2 minutes, 46 seconds. Ozzy, however, disliked the song at first. As he later explained: "I thought it was too pop. We were a band that refused to conform to a commercial formula, and when we did 'Paranoid', I rebelled against it."

Despite the singer's protests, 'Paranoid' was issued as a single on July 17, 1970 – two months ahead of the album. By August, it had reached Number 4 on the UK chart. In the wake of this success, the album – originally titled *War Pigs* – was hastily renamed *Paranoid*. But there was no time to change the album artwork – a somewhat bizarre visual interpretation of 'War Pigs', featuring a blurry, wild-eyed warrior figure in a motorcycle crash helmet, brandishing a sword and shield.

'War Pigs' was chosen as the album's thunderous opening salvo. Originally named Walpurgis after an ancient European spring festival, it is a furious anti-war tirade, which had a powerful impact at a time when the US was still embroiled in the Vietnam conflict. As Butler explained to journalist Mick Wall: "We used to play American military bases in Germany, and I'd talk to soldiers who'd tell me these horrendous stories about Vietnam. That's where the lyrics came from."

There was also an echo of Vietnam in Butler's lyrics for the heroin blues 'Hand Of Doom'. And another song destined to become a Black Sabbath classic was 'Iron Man', a sci-fi horror fantasy, with Iommi bending notes to fearsome effect before the leaden riff kicks in.

In contrast, 'Planet Caravan' has a hazy, dreamlike ambience, a tale of astral travel with a trippy, spaced-out groove. And to end an album on which the central themes are death, destruction and insanity, there is a song that provides a little levity. Butler's lyrics describe an incident that happened during a UK tour. Following a gig in the

Opposite: An original concert handbill from the performance of Black Sabbath at the Audimax der Freien Universitat, Berlin. The concert took place on June 26, 1970. They were supported by Frumpy.

"I THOUGHT IT WAS TOO POP... WHEN WE DID 'PARANOID', I REBELLED AGAINST IT."

Ozzy Osbourne

LIVE
The Magic Of
Black Sabbath

Eine knallharte Rhythmusgruppe, Terry Butler und Bill Ward, liefert das Fundament für die besessenen Improvisationen der Gitarre Tony Lommi's und die elektrisierende Blues-stimme von Ossie Osbourne, dessen wilde Schreie aus dem Inferno eines Hexensabbats zu kommen scheinen. Die Live-Auftritte dieser Gruppe sind ein Erlebnis.

and groups
Frumpy (ex City Preachers) Hairy Chapter

Berlin   Audimax der Freien Universität
Henry-Ford-Bau, Garystr. 35

Freitag, den 26. Juni, 20.00 Uhr

Karten im Vorverkauf bei

Bote & Bock, Europa-Center
Theaterkasse Kiosk am Zoo
„   Sasse am Café Zuntz
„   Maaß, Kurfürstendamm 215
„   Wildbad-Kiosk
Restkarten an der Abendkasse

Sie erreichen das Audimax der F U (Henry-Ford-Bau, Garystr. 35)
über U-Bahn-Station Thiel-Platz, Linie Krumme Lanke und die Bus-Linien 10 u. 11

"WE WANT PEOPLE TO LISTEN TO US, NOT TRY TO TOUCH US. I WAS REALLY TERRIFIED..."

Ozzy Osbourne

South West of England, Butler had been in a phone box making a call to Sabbath's manager, complaining that the band didn't have enough money to buy petrol to get them home to Birmingham. As he talked, he noticed a gang of skinheads loitering outside the phone box. Butler was attacked but managed to fend them off. And had the last laugh when he named this song 'Fairies Wear Boots'.

Released on September 18, 1970, just seven months after their first album, *Paranoid* confirmed Black Sabbath as a major force in a new rock era, topping the UK chart and hitting Number 12 in the US. The album would have a huge influence on future generations of heavy bands.

And just as *Paranoid* would be acknowledged as the definitive Black Sabbath album, so its title track would become their signature song. Ozzy didn't much care for it when it was first recorded, but at every gig he has played since then – with Sabbath and without – he has sung this song. "I couldn't go onstage and not do 'Paranoid'," he said.

There were many landmark rock albums released in 1970, from *After The Gold Rush* by Neil Young to the Beatles' swansong *Let It Be* and the solo albums *McCartney*, *John Lennon/Plastic Ono Band* and George Harrison's *All Things Must Pass*. At the heavier end of rock, there was the Who's *Live At Leeds*, Free's *Fire And Water*, Led Zeppelin *III*, and *Deep Purple In Rock*.

But Black Sabbath delivered two classic albums in that year. And with *Paranoid*, they had created their masterpiece. Arguably, the greatest heavy metal album of them all.

Left: Is there something in Bill's direct gaze which hints at the demons which would plague him for the rest of his life?

Below: A ticket to the "Marquay" Club event in July 1, 1970. Black Sabbath were supported by Adolphus Rebirth and Blue Blood.

MARQUAY CLUB
TORQUAY TOWN HALL

BLACK MAGIC with
Black Sabbath

Adolphus Rebirth :: **Blue Blood**

Wednesday, 1st July, 1970

8 p.m.—1 a.m.   Bar till 12.30 a.m.   Pass-Outs

Admit One 10/-

№ 00339

WAR PIGS

War Pigs was the proposed album title, as well as a phenomenal opening track. Described in *Guitar World* as "the greatest HM song ever", it begins with the immortal couplet: "Generals gathered in their masses/Just like witches at black masses."

The song started life as 'Walpurgis' or, as Geezer puts it, "Satan's Christmas thing." But because of the furore surrounding Black Sabbath and their alleged involvement in black magic, they decided to re-write the lyrics, and 'War Pigs' became a protest song, condemning the war in Vietnam and the hypocrisies of the politicians and the propagandists who sent young men off to die in the jungles.

In typical Sabbath style, the "war pigs" reap what they've sown when Judgement Day finds them crawling on their knees, begging forgiveness, while "Satan, laughing, spreads his wings". Legend has it that Sabbath heard horror stories about the war from soldiers they were entertaining at an American Air Force base, but Ozzy, while conceding that the song is about Vietnam, contends: "We knew nothing about Vietman. It's just an anti-war song."

The record company refused to accept *War Pigs* as the album title due to American sensitivities over Vietnam, and settled on *Paranoid* instead.

However, there was no time to change the sleeve artwork, so *Paranoid* is rather ineffectually illustrated by a man running out of a forest with a helmet, sword and shield.

Bonham, Ward's drinking buddy. Ward told Steven Rosen: "John was a big fan of Black Sabbath... he would play on my kit and he would make the kit sing...

"He liked what I did with the hi-hat. But he was always jiving me about how I had too many drums and said, 'These (Zeppelin) bastards won't let me have any drums.'"

Bonham particularly liked 'Supernaut' and 'Cornucopia', both from the *Vol 4* album.

PARANOID

Estimates range between five and 30 minutes. That's how long it took for Black Sabbath (or Ward's handy fifth member) to write and arrange the band's most famous anthem. It was a last-minute effort, a quick space-filler at the end of the main recording sessions, and it was perfect.

Ozzy said: "I remember Rodger Bain (the producer) saying: 'We need three or four minutes to finish the album.' So Tony came up with the riff, I came up with the melody, Geezer wrote the lyrics and it was done within 10 minutes. Geezer didn't even know what the word "paranoid" meant, but people were always calling him that, so he made it the title of the song."

Ozzy also suggested that, "The best songs always happen that way. You can sit down and plan and fucking work it out, but it's those

quicklies that turn out the best." And he added: "Considering we recorded it in three-and-a-half minutes, it's not bad."

Released as a single in August 1970, "Paranoid" reached number four in the UK and stayed in the chart for 18 weeks. In the US, three months later, it registered at number 61.

While *Paranoid* is still the people's favourite Sabbath album, "Paranoid" the single remains highly rated in polls of greatest-ever rock tracks, and in 1995, it won Tony Iommi a *Kerrang!* award for "Best Guitar Riff Ever".

But its success 25 years earlier came as a mixed blessing, attracting a new, young and very excitable crowd to Sabbath gigs. Ozzy said of one gig at Portsmouth: "There were kids rushing down the front and girls screaming and grabbing us. We couldn't believe it...

"We don't need fans like those. We'll just have to grin and bear them and they'll go away. We're not changing our stage act to please the kids who just bought the single."

Problems were also reported in Newcastle, where the crowd surged uncontrollably on to the stage, destroying a PA speaker and a bass drum microphone and thieving Ward's drumsticks and cymbals.

Ozzy said at the time: "If it means us having to give up putting out singles, then we will. We want people to listen to us, not try to touch us. I was really terrified, shocked out of my mind."

IRON MAN

Another Sabbath monster, the melancholic "Iron Man", with its massive riff, also became an immediate crowd favourite. "I am Iron Man," warns Ozzy on the record, acting out his dramatic role to the full.

It was Ozzy who suggested the title to an inspired Geezer Butler. Geezer, who was responsible for almost all of the band's lyrics, said: "Ozzy might come up with a line at the time when we were writing the stuff, such as 'Iron Man'. He was humming along and said, 'Iron Man'."

Geezer continues: "I wrote it about this guy who's blasted off into space and sees the future of the world, which isn't very good. Then he goes through a magnetic storm on the way back and is turned into iron.

"He's trying to warn everyone about the future, but he can't speak, so everyone is taking the mickey out of him all the time, and he just doesn't care in the end.

"He goes a bit barmy and decides to get his revenge by killing people," added Ozzy. "He tries to do good, but in the end, it turns into bad."

Released in the US in January 1972, "Iron Man" reached Number 52, and it remained the group's highest-charting single in America.

HAND OF DOOM

Unusually for Black Sabbath, the lyrics wagged a finger at themselves.

There had been a tradition of alcohol and drugs, mainly dope, around the band from their earliest days. And in years to come, with money no object, they would be unrivalled in their capacity to devour illicit substances, with stories abounding of days-long marathons and supplies of cocaine being delivered to the door in cereal cartons.

Bill Ward has admitted that his most enduring memory of the period leading up the *Paranoid* album is of taking drugs, specifically hash. He was also a fearless drinker, regularly out on the rampage with a voracious John Bonham.

Tony Iommi has also recalled the excessive drinking during this time which went on for years to come. His bandmates, he said, were often so drunk they left him on his own, effectively giving him the responsibility of delivering an album's worth of new ideas. He didn't disappoint – and he was no saint himself.

Iommi would later suffer from memory loss relating to his own recreational pursuits. He recalled that pills, all sorts of pills, came into the picture around the time of *Paranoid*. And strong, new alliances with acid and cocaine were just around the corner.

However, the warnings dished out sternly in "Hand Of Doom" speak of heavier stuff altogether. Graphically depicting a mainlining junkie, the lyrics urge: "Push the needle in/Face death's sickly grin" before climaxing, vividly, with an overdose.

While the song ostensibly centres on an army veteran trying to blot out the horrors of Vietnam, it's widely believed that the drugs references were to some extent personal, confessional, even accusatory.

The tragedy unfolds as suspense, drama and tempos build within a harrowing soundtrack – one credited with spawning the sub-genre of doom metal, which depends on "heaviness, darkness, sadness, depression and melancholy".

Undeniably, "Hand Of Doom" is a textbook mixture of these requirements, along with other tracks from the band's repertoire. Sabbath were simply the first of the forefathers.

FAIRIES WEAR BOOTS

Skinhead thugs were attracting a lot of criticism in the UK at this time, particularly from Black Sabbath who had fallen victim to a gang attack.

This reportedly happened on the night of the Newcastle stage invasion, with the band being set upon as they walked through the streets after the show. Tony Iommi sustained painful arm injuries in the fracas, and the band were forced to call off their next gig.

In the pre-politically correct world of the time, Sabbath retaliated by abusing the boot-boys in the way which would most insult them – as "fairies".

Varying the pace and style before launching into a solid and satisfyingly raucous charge, Ozzy relishes a lyric which sneers: "Fairy boots were dancin' with a dwarf/All right now!"

The song is eager to incorporate another hint at drugs consumption with descriptions of a visit to the doctor: "He said, 'Son, son, you've gone too far/Cause smokin' and trippin' is all that you do.'"

Other tracks on the album are the almost balladic "Planet Caravan", which is slow, evocative, spacey and a little unnerving, with Ozzy's vocals treated with some primitive, electronic device; the thuddingly morbid "Electric Funeral", and the guitar and drum showcase of "Rat Salad".

Opposite: A serious Sabbath pose during a photo shoot in Copenhagen, Denmark, on December 12, 1970.

PROFILE
TOMMY IOMMI

THERE HAS NEVER BEEN A BLACK SABBATH WITHOUT TONY IOMMI.
FOR THE BEST PART OF 40 YEARS, THE LEGENDARY GUITARIST
HAS BEEN THE BAND'S LEADER AND DRIVING FORCE. AND THAT
DETERMINATION IS WHAT HAS ALSO SUSTAINED HIM THROUGH THE
BIGGEST CHALLENGE OF HIS LIFE – HIS ONGOING BATTLE WITH CANCER.

In the epic saga of Black Sabbath there is one dominant figure. Throughout all the years and the many different line-ups of the band, Tony Iommi is the sole constant. Black Sabbath has been at the centre of his entire adult life, and equally, it is his creative genius that has made Sabbath the most influential heavy metal band of all time.

He was born on Thursday, February 19, 1948 in Heathfield Road Hospital in Birmingham. The only child of Italian immigrants, he was named after his father Anthony Frank Iommi.

In his formative years as a teenager, growing up in an impoverished neighbourhood of Britain's second city, Iommi learned the hard way that he had to be tough to survive. "The area where I lived was quite rough," he recalled. "There were gangs, a lot of fighting in the streets. People would beat the shit out of you if you didn't do it to them. That's how it was."

Music would provide an escape from gang culture. Inspired by British rock 'n' roll stars Hank Marvin and The Shadows, Iommi started playing guitar, left-handed, devoting all his spare time to practising, instead of going out and getting into trouble. Music also offered a route out of the mundane industrial jobs to which he felt predestined, like so many of his peers. At 16, he joined his first semi-professional band, the Rockin' Chevrolets. But then came the accident that might have ended the dream.

Iommi was on his last day of work at a sheet metal factory when his hand was caught in machinery and he lost the tips of two fingers. When his injuries were first assessed, doctors had advised him to forget about playing guitar. "But I believed I could do it," he said. "And I did. I proved them wrong, didn't I?"

With the use of artificial fingertips, which he designed and made himself, he devised a new way of playing – albeit with some limitations. As he explained: "There are certain chords I can't play. You can't feel the strings, so you have to play by ear." But as he developed this unorthodox style, Iommi was able to create a sound that was unique among rock guitarists. And it was a sound that would effectively define heavy metal across the decades.

Black Sabbath's whole career has been built on Tony Iommi's riffs. This band, like every other, is the sum of its parts, but as Ozzy once said: "Without Tony's riffs, we wouldn't have had a fucking chance in hell of doing anything." Ozzy also acknowledges that Black Sabbath is in essence Iommi's band. In 2013, Ozzy said: "Tony has always been the leader. And he's still the boss."

Since he co-founded Black Sabbath in 1969, Iommi has been married four times, but has had only one band – in reality, Heaven & Hell was Sabbath in all but name. Leading Sabbath for so many years has proven difficult at times. He told *Classic Rock*: "The lowest point was trying to hold the pieces together in the 80s and 90s. Geezer had gone, Ozzy, Bill, Ronnie… I didn't have any friends in the band anymore. But I never thought about giving up. I just couldn't let go. If I'd turned my back on the band, I'd have regretted it."

For many of those years, Iommi had longed to make a new album with the original Black Sabbath. "I always thought there was a chance of it happening," he said. When Osbourne and Butler both finally agreed to reunite for *13,* he was saddened that Bill Ward declined to participate. But the making of that album was of huge importance to Iommi – not simply on an artistic level, but also in terms of how it helped him through the darkest days of his life.

When he was diagnosed with lymphoma in 2012, Iommi feared the worst. Less than two years earlier, Ronnie James Dio had also died from cancer, albeit a different form. Iommi was undergoing chemotherapy treatment during the recording of the Sabbath album. And in an interview with *Classic Rock*, he revealed the extent to which the process of making music aided his psychological and emotional condition.

"I needed something to focus on," he said. "And that's what this album gave me. With cancer, the worst thing you can do is sit around thinking about it all the time. So to work on this album – to play with the band and have a laugh with them – it was all good medicine for me."

In 2013, Iommi looked back on his career and said simply: "There have been two major albums in my life." For very different reasons, the albums he chose were these: "*Paranoid* and *13.*"

Opposite: The godfather of heavy metal himself; had Iommi never injured his fingertips, who knows where guitar music would have ended up?

"IF I'D TURNED MY BACK ON THE BAND, I'D HAVE REGRETTED IT."

Tony Iommi

Black Sabbath's first gig in America had been a sobering experience. In the autumn of 1970, the band arrived in New York as the rising stars of British rock, with a Number 1 album back at home. But on November 1, when they arrived at the venue for their debut US performance, they got a nasty surprise.

Ungano's was a grungy basement joint on New York's Staten Island. And as Tony Iommi recalled to writer Mick Wall: "It was a shit-hole. A

little farty club. I thought, 'Fucking hell, this is America?'"

But their disappointment didn't last long. Just nine days later, Sabbath opened for the Faces at the prestigious Fillmore East theatre in Manhattan, and the audience greeted them as heroes. "The crowd

Above and opposite: Black Sabbath on tour and Ozzy onstage in 1971, the year when *Master Of Reality* was released.

"IT WAS... A LITTLE FARTY CLUB. I THOUGHT: 'FUCKING HELL, THIS IS AMERICA?"

Tony Iommi

went absolutely mental," Geezer Butler said. In fact, Sabbath was a hard act to follow – Butler claims that during the Faces' set, people were throwing bottles at singer Rod Stewart. And by word of mouth, the news travelled fast. When Sabbath returned to the Fillmore East four months later, they were the headline act for two sold-out shows.

Sabbath made quick work of breaking America. On that first visit in November 1970, they played mostly support slots: for Alice Cooper at the Whisky A Go-Go in Los Angeles, and for the James Gang at the Fillmore West in San Francisco. By the end of that month-long tour, they headlined two theatre shows in Detroit and one in New Jersey, where their opening act was Steel Mill, featuring a young Bruce Springsteen.

But on their second American tour in early 1971, heralded by the US release of the *Paranoid* album, Sabbath were fast-tracked into headlining in arenas, and played to five-figure audiences. As Bill Ward recalled: "When we got to LA and did the Forum, this big, 15,000-seater, I realized we were involved in something big." When the tour ended on April 2 with another sold-out arena show at the Philadelphia Spectrum, *Paranoid* was at Number 12 on the US *Billboard* chart.

Work on the band's third album had already begun in January at Island Studios in London. Again, Rodger Bain was the producer. New songs were in short supply. After two albums, the band had nothing left over. And in the midst of a hectic touring schedule, there had been little time for writing. But when they returned to England in April, they had just enough material to complete the album: six songs, to which were added two instrumental pieces that Iommi conjured up in the studio. In total, there were just 34 minutes of music. But no matter: the album, titled *Master Of Reality*, was another classic and another huge hit. And it would prove to be one of the most influential albums in the entire history of rock and roll.

"*Master Of Reality* was an experiment," Iommi told *Classic Rock*. "On songs like 'Children Of The Grave' and 'Into The Void', we tuned down three semitones for a bigger sound, with more depth." The result was the heaviest album the band ever made.

The tone is set by the dense and sluggish opening track 'Sweet Leaf', their homage to marijuana, which begins with a hacking cough from Iommi, recorded after he'd had a go on "a bloody big joint" handed to him by Ozzy. 'Children Of The Grave', powered by one of Iommi's greatest riffs, is a Cold War protest song – in a sense, a natural successor to 'War Pigs'. 'After Forever' is Butler's meditation on religion, in stark contrast to the band's reputation as Satanists (although the song would arouse controversy due to the line: 'Would you like to see the Pope on the end of a rope?'). And there are moments of quiet beauty, too – in the two instrumental tracks, 'Embryo' and 'Orchid', and in what Iommi calls Black Sabbath's "first love song", 'Solitude'.

Released on July 21, 1971, *Master Of Reality* did not repeat the success of *Paranoid* in the UK. It peaked at Number 5. But it was Sabbath's first album to break into the US Top 10. And when the band

hit the road in America that summer for a 38-date tour, they were playing to tens of thousands of people, night after night. On only two dates on the tour did Sabbath open for another band – and that band was Led Zeppelin.

In a review for America's premier rock magazine *Rolling Stone*, critic Lester Bangs hailed *Master Of Reality* as the band's best album yet. "Rock and roll has always been noise," Bangs wrote, "and Black Sabbath have boiled that noise to its resinous essence."

Over time, *Master Of Reality* would have a pivotal influence on new genres of heavy music, such as stoner rock and doom metal. In 1971, it blew America wide open for Black Sabbath. And it was at that point that they were introduced to a new drug. Something that could take them even higher...

Opposite: Ozzy on tour and enjoying the high life.

Above: A fitting spot for a Sabbath photo shoot: the band looks moody in the overgrown grounds of an old church.

Next spread: Sabbath playing the Paradiso Theatre. Amsterdam, on December 4, 1971. They were supported by English blues-rock band Ten Years After.

SWEET LEAF

The track, and the album, open with the sounds of coughing, courtesy of Tony Iommi who had just enjoyed a lengthy draw from a bong.

The band believed they owed it to the public to spread the good news about grass, and since "Sweet Leaf" was written for this specific purpose, Iommi's coughs erupted with perfect timing as the tapes began to roll.

Ozzy has described the origins of the song, which is heavily, densely unhurried and also noteworthy for a sensational guitar riff.

"I'd just come back from Dublin," said Ozzy, "and I had these Sweet Afton cigarettes you can only get in Ireland and it had on them, 'It's the sweetest leaf that you can taste.'

"Geezer wondered, 'What can we write this one about?' and I just looked at it and went, 'Sweet leaf – yeah!'"

Bill Ward talked about the track to Steven Rosen. He said: "That was very necessary to do at the time. Letting people know about marijuana – that's what it's about."

The lyrics take the form of a love song to the aromatic plant which, said Sabbath, was a cure-all. It could fill empty lives, lift depression and help its users feel "free" and "clear". In conclusion, the song urges: "Come on now, try it out/Straight people don't know what you're about."

This was a favourite of Ozzy, who carried on playing it live throughout his solo career. He recalled: "I used to do a lot of grass and LSD back in the Black Sabbath days. One time I was out of my tree for a week talking to horses. And the weird thing was, they were talking back to me."

More recently, he reflected: "I used to smoke all the time when I was younger. It seems to have become so strong nowadays – I hate the feeling. We used to smoke stuff that would make us giggle and give us the munchies. Now it's like being on acid – when's it gonna end?"

AFTER FOREVER

Geezer Butler's ode to Christianity did little to extricate Black Sabbath from their devilish associations, if that was indeed his intention. It simply managed to upset more people – the church authorities, who condemned it as blasphemous, and the Satanic community, who contended that Sabbath had sold out to God!

Still, it sent out a confusing message to fans, still arguing the contradictions. Had Geezer penned a supremely ironic dismissal of organized religion or was this some sort of spiritual insurance policy for a band beset by death threats and evil spells? Had he written, fictitiously or factually, of someone else's experience, in the first person? Was he opening a debate? Was he mixing it? Or was he really a God-fearing individual who felt it was time to bear witness, to set the record straight after writing so voluminously about the dark side?

Some people believe that this, remarkably, was the case. Certainly, in all of his references to "After Forever", Butler has talked extremely seriously about the creative achievements of his lyric.

In contrast, there is nothing terribly sensitive about the track's big musical features, the crushing momentum and Iommi's enduring riff. One schoolboy rhyme follows another as Ozzy gives voice to Geezer's assertions that he had seen the truth and the light, had changed his ways and was certainly not about to join the lost souls who are

"Lonely and scared at the end of our days". He goes on to lambast those unfortunates who fail to realize that "God is the only way to love", or who are afraid to invite ridicule by acknowledging this. Finally, thunders the song: "I think it was true it was people like you/That crucified Christ".

"Isn't all this Christian folderol just the flip side of the Luciferian creed they commenced with and look back on balefully in "Lord Of This World"?" queried *Rolling Stone*'s Lester Bangs.

In a work titled "Satanism and Heavy Metal: The Confusion Continues", author Matt C Paradise proposed: "Ozzy Osbourne, then lead singer for the band, could have very well been the first Christian rocker. Within the lyrics of their songs, they expressed Christian concepts of (the Christian) God vs Satan (Black Sabbath), reconciliation with Christian beliefs ("After Forever"), a plea to Jesus for help (a common theme in Sabbath songs, most notably "The Thrill Of It All"), Satan being the motivator for war ("War Pigs") and many others.

"Of course, Sabbath also sang about degenerate, hippie topics as well, but even hippies have a love for master/slave relationships (drugs and Christian God being two of them)."

Avoiding the tricky topic of master/slave relationships, writer George Starostin ventured: "The fact that bassist Geezer Butler's lyrics were ultimately shallow, stupid, banal and even ridiculous, and, above all, were mostly directed against Satan – though it took some time to understand it – didn't help (the band). Even when they made the lyrics sound Christian, they were still treated as a new, horrendous brand of anti-Christs."

He added: "I have absolutely no doubt that these lyrics were totally tongue-in-cheek, attempted as a joke in the face of the church."

The last word goes to Ozzy, Geezer's mouthpiece for "After Forever", stating firmly in 1990: "I believe in God. I don't believe in the devil. I am not a devil worshipper. My kids do not sleep in the attic, hanging upside down on rafters."

CHILDREN OF THE GRAVE

Despite its gruesome title, the surging, riff-driven "Children Of The Grave" holds out a certain, Lennon-esque optimism and declares a war on evil. It calls upon the young generation to grow up resisting the xenophobia of their parents' world and to fight for peace and a future free of conflict and nuclear aggression until "Love comes flowing through".

"Show the world that love is still alive!" counsels Ozzy, before issuing a stark, concluding warning: "You must be brave/Or you children of today are children of the grave/Yeah!"

The singer later shared his views of the song: "My interpretation of that is that in every generation, there's a new revolution. Every generation hates something about the current generation. It was our punk song, if you like."

LORD OF THIS WORLD

"That was our one and only Satan song," declared Geezer Butler, conveniently overlooking a goodly proportion of Black Sabbath's repertoire. "It's about old Nick."

Old Nick was treated to a suitable Sabbath work-out, one of those murderously slow–paced spectaculars like "Sweet Leaf", that moves

from one mood to another with showers of showmanship from Tony Iommi and outbursts of spontaneous jamming. A continuing fan favourite, "Lord Of This World" is as short on lyrics as it is long on musical theatrics.

"Lord of this world, evil possessor/Lord of this world, he's your confessor now," sings Ozzy in his final summation.

INTO THE VOID

Again putting some distance between themselves and the morbid, macabre and occult obsessions for which they had become notorious, Black Sabbath returned to the themes they had visited on "Children Of The Grave", rejecting the wars, bigotry, brainwashing, wickedness and pollution of the world and proposing an escape by rocket ship to a place where "Love is there to stay". "Leave the earth to Satan and his slaves/Leave them to their future in the grave!" cries Ozzy in the rip-roaring "Into The Void". Lyrically as well as musically, Sabbath were clearly ready to move on.

Other tracks on the album are the tiny instrumentals "Embryo" and "Orchid", and the hypnotic, despairing ballad "Solitude", arranged with flutes and echo.

Above: An uncharacteristically subdued Ozzy is captured candidly by a photographer in 1972.

VOL. 4
(1972)

IN 1972, WITH THEIR POPULARITY IN AMERICA SOARING, BLACK SABBATH
CHOSE TO STAY THERE TO RECORD THEIR FOURTH ALBUM. SETTLING IN LOS
ANGELES, THEY CREATED *VOL. 4* AMID A BLIZZARD OF COCAINE. "WE WERE
OUT OF OUR MINDS," OZZY SAID. THE ALBUM IS A MONUMENT TO THAT EXCESS.

The first time that Tony Iommi took cocaine was in the autumn of 1971. Black Sabbath were appearing at the Los Angeles Forum, and in the moments before the band went on stage, Iommi was offered the drug by a member of the road crew. He was told that it would help him to concentrate. It did more than that. In Iommi's mind, his playing that night was out of this world.

By the time Sabbath returned to LA in May 1972, to begin work on their fourth album, it wasn't only Iommi that was hooked on coke. They were all at it. And nowhere was cocaine more freely available than in LA, the music business capital of America.

When Sabbath arrived in LA, they were once again struggling for new material. The year had begun with another busy touring schedule, first in the UK, then in the US and Canada with progressive rock band Yes as the support act. When they got back to the UK, their attempts at writing and rehearsing new songs proved frustrating. More often than not, Iommi would be left to work alone as the others nipped off to the local pub. They would be gone for hours. And if they did bother to return, they'd be plastered. Days would pass into weeks, with little achieved. So when the band's management suggested a change of location to LA, Iommi readily agreed.

In LA, they could start afresh. The studios there were cheaper, too. And they loved LA – for the sunshine, the women, the drugs. Especially the drugs...

The band moved into a rented mansion in the upscale neighbourhood of Bel Air, with a large pool and panoramic views of the city. And there, the new songs came together quickly – the creative process accelerated by high-grade cocaine delivered daily in sealed boxes the size of cereal packets.

One day, they nearly got busted. They were gathered in the mansion's TV room, sitting around a table laden with a small mountain of coke,

Above and opposite: Postcards of Black Sabbath performing on stage at the Royal Albert Hall, London on February 17, 1972. The concert was part of the band's Master Of Reality tour.

"WE HAD SUCH A GOOD TIME, WE DIDN'T WANT IT TO END."

Tony Iommi

when Bill Ward accidentally pressed a button that activated an alarm. Within a few minutes, several police cars had arrived. In a panic, the four band members hoovered up as much of the coke as they could, and flushed the remainder down the toilet. The police found nothing, and left after Ward explained his mistake. After the last police car had disappeared, Iommi was straight on the phone to his dealer.

They did, however, dial down the excess when they set about recording the album at The Record Plant studios. This time, Rodger Bain would not be required. The band elected to produce the album themselves, although their manager Patrick Meehan, who had replaced Jim Simpson in 1970, was credited as co-producer.

The influence of cocaine was prevalent throughout *Vol. 4*. It was most explicit on the song 'Snowblind', which was originally intended to be the title track. In the style of 'Sweet Leaf', it was a eulogy to their new drug of choice. But as Iommi recalled, cocaine also emboldened the band to try new ideas.

There was a piano in the mansion, which Iommi played during many sleepless nights. From this, he developed the Beatles-inspired ballad 'Changes'. And there were other tracks on which the band stretched out. The heaviest song on the album, 'Supernaut', ended with a funky coda, and 'Wheels Of Confusion' bordered on progressive rock.

The weirdest track on *Vol. 4* was formed under the influence of a different drug. The brief instrumental 'FX' was recorded when the band were stoned on marijuana, all of them nearly naked as they danced around the studio room, hitting Iommi's guitar to create a series of echoing notes. But the essence of this album was crystallized in a dedication printed on the back cover: "We wish to thank the great COKE-Cola Company."

Vol. 4 was released on September 25, 1972. It reached Number 8 in the UK, Number 13 in the US. And for an album borne out of drug-induced mania, the review in *Rolling Stone* was suitably gonzoid. Writer Tom Clark described the sound of 'Wheels Of Confusion' as "like some giant prehistoric plant learning how to walk… right over your house… so boogie while you can." 'Supernaut' inspired "a vision of electronic buffalo ranches on Uranus." And so on. He concluded: "The Sabs are genius."

Vol. 4 is one of the definitive and classic Black Sabbath albums. And for Tony Iommi, it will always be remembered for the fun they had making it. "We had such a good time," he said. "We didn't want it to end."

Opposite: The two faces of Bill Ward. The tortured artist, wrestling with the forces that drove him to be one of the finest rock drummers in the world…

Right: …and the relaxed, happy-go-lucky clown of the band who routinely submitted to practical jokes. Who would you set on fire if you were in Black Sabbath?

CHANGES

The album kicks in with the epic "Wheels Of Confusion", an unorthodox amalgamation of changing tempos, solos and a simply monumental riff from Tony Iommi, while the following, powerful "Tomorrow's Dream", much shorter and certainly more mainstream, was released as a single, the first since "Paranoid", to little excitement in the chart. So far so Sabbath.

But three tracks in, they rang some "Changes". Tinkling piano keys underpin a hugely melodic and emotional performance from Ozzy as the band weaves an irresistible air of melancholy to create what has been pinpointed as the world's first power ballad.

Like the two songs which precede it, "Changes" is an unhappy proposition, a simplistic story of lost love and regret: "Wish I could go back and change these years".

The unidentified break-up (rumoured in some circles to describe Bill Ward's first divorce) is attributed to the wicked ways of the world – a possible reference to the life of wine, women and song that the band were living during their big Hollywood adventure.

It's a track that has sharply divided long-time Sabbath fans. Some would like to write it out of the history books forever; others contend that it remains the loveliest song they've ever heard from the band.

SUPERNAUT

No complaints here, as Sabbath weigh in with a hectic energy that finds Tony Iommi playing hard and fast in what is probably his first recorded instance of high-speed guitar riffing. The sheer magnitude of the song, the combination of juggernaut aggression and catchy hooks – plus a drum solo! – puts "Supernaut" up there among the tracks most loved by fans to this day.

It's generally interpreted as a drug song, a selfishly worded defence of some illegal substance. It could be about acid – the assertion that "I want to touch the sun/But I don't need to fly" is not the only fanciful pronouncement. It could be about heroin, the wares of a "distant man" seen to be hovering around the lyrics waving a spoon. And, of course, it could be about cocaine, just because of the superhuman assurance pervading the lyric and because we know how devotedly the members of Black Sabbath adored their white stuff in the good old days of 1972.

Flying in the face of their Satanic reputation and the ambiguous, Christian sentiments of "After Forever", the song starkly decrees, "Got no religion, don't need no friends", a theme which would recur, in greater detail, later on in the album to compound the mysteries of the Black Sabbath spiritual soap opera.

SNOWBLIND

This was to be the name of the LP before yet another intervention from the record label. With the decision to add an upside-down cross to the artwork for *Black Sabbath*, executives had aimed to heighten the band's notoriety. But in forbidding "War Pigs" as a title for the album eventually called *Paranoid* and by then banning "Snowblind", the boardroom flexed some serious, censorious muscle: Sabbath were being firmly guided away from controversy.

"Snowblind" – an unequivocal reference to cocaine – was axed in favour of the anaemic title *Vol 4*.

There was no huge revolt from the band, but they did strike back with a couple of blows against the empire. The sleeve acknowledgements thank the "COKE-Cola" company. And Ozzy blurted out "cocaine" at the end of every verse of the "Snowblind" track. Ordered to remove the offending word, he nevertheless smuggled it onto the recording by means of a whisper, determined to immortalize a lifestyle that revolved around coke while at the same time admitting to journalists that he thought he was "going nuts".

He said recently, "I remember that when you'd run out of cocaine, you'd be scratching the carpet for anything that resembled the white stuff. It could be dog shit and you'd be putting it up your nose: 'Oh, look, there's a rock!'"

Matter-of-factly, he stated: "We were doing tons of the fucking stuff."

While the group storm into the song like the undisputed heavyweight champions they were, changing pace with a bruising and unsmiling authority, Ozzy gives forth in a stark, almost chanting vocal about the satisfying numbness of "Feeling happy in my vein/Icicles within my brain". The lyrics speak of a strange and self-contained comfort, but the imagery is largely cold and lonely – not the most persuasive argument for a new hobby – and a defiant tone again enters: "Don't tell me that it's doing me wrong/You're the one who's really a loser..." These days, Ozzy would probably disagree with the sentiment, while defending to the death his right to have sung it.

CORNUCOPIA

Geezer Butler was spurred into action by a radio report that "only" 25 men had been killed in the Vietnam war that week. Seizing upon "cornucopia" as a keyword for abundance and prosperity, his lyrics bitterly attacked society's consumerism and heartlessness. It was all very admirable: a band with a conscience.

But back in the early Seventies, when first-division heavy metal was a place of unparalleled excess and self-indulgence, it seems hypocritical for any rock star to criticize the expensive habits of others.

Sex, drugs and rock'n'roll could well be said to be the group's own equivalent of the "Little toys, fast sports cars and motor noise" so scathingly highlighted in the song, and for all of his good intentions, Geezer's focus on symbols rather than symptoms rang hollow, especially since Black Sabbath were in just as much of a "plastic place" as those criticized in his lyrics.

Little of this was of any interest to Bill Ward, whose problems with "Cornucopia" were closer to home. He loathed the track, which is a heavy-duty Sabbath rocker, loaded with time and tempo changes, and Bill could not get to grips with the patterns. The band returned to England to finish up some bits and pieces for the album, "Cornucopia" among them. Bill was on booze and coke round the clock, was fed up in the studio, and was developing a mental block, a "terrible resentment" about "Cornucopia".

Something about Bill's friendship with Alvin Lee was also causing friction in the ranks. Ward's bandmates – including his usual ally, Ozzy – unanimously decided that he should go home, since he wasn't serving any useful purpose in the studio. Unfortunately, Bill didn't have a home to go to, since he'd been on the road so much, he hadn't reckoned he needed one. Bill trudged off into the night with his wife, profoundly shocked and fearful for his job. The pair gravitated to Geezer Butler's house and spent the night sleeping under coats in his back garden.

"That was the very first indication that there was a change, because that had never happened before," said Ward to Steven Rosen. "It had all been fine. Suddenly, here in *Vol 4* there was a change, a definite change.

"It really scared me. And it was the first time that any band member had ever been rebuked. It hurt. I mean, they didn't want me in the studio. Sometimes we'd have cross words, but that was the first time I actually felt like I'd blown it." Eventually, Ward completed his drum part to everyone's satisfaction.

UNDER THE SUN

The chunky guitar riffs, the solos, the drum fills and the thrill of Ozzy in full flight conform to the original Sabbath blueprint. But the lyrics utter a complete rejection of everything that had gone before.

"Well I don't want no demon to tell me what it's all about…" Geezer didn't want no black magic wizard either, or no preacher telling him about God. He didn't want to know about the afterlife, and he didn't want to know the vast majority of his fellow-human beings. "I just believe in myself," he wrote, "Cos no one else is true."

If the lyrics are to be taken literally, this all appears to have arisen from some drug-induced revelation: he had opened the door, he assured us. He had released his mind, realized that life was "one big overdose" and decided that from then on, he would follow his own path and to hell with everyone else.

It must have been one of those moments; a more familiar Geezer would re-emerge on the next Black Sabbath album.

Other tracks on the album are the oddly experimental, some might say dispensable: "FX", which runs to just over a minute and a half; the instrumental "Laguna Sunrise", with its acoustic guitars and string section; and the battering "St Vitus Dance", an unusual, new take on the age-old story of women chasing rock stars for their money.

Above: Vol. 4-era Ozzy, hair whipping in a trademark fashion, performs to an adoring crowd in Manchester, 1972.

PROFILE
OZZY OSBOURNE

HE IS THE EX-CONVICT WHO ENDED UP A MULTI-MILLIONAIRE, THE ROCK
STAR WHO BROKE ALL RECORDS FOR DRINKING AND DRUG TAKING,
THE MADMAN WHO BIT THE HEADS OFF DEFENCELESS ANIMALS. MOST
IMPORTANT OF ALL, OZZY OSBOURNE IS THE ORIGINAL SINGER FOR
THE GREATEST HEAVY METAL BAND THAT HAS EVER EXISTED.

'I've had a blessed life, man," Ozzy Osbourne said in 1991. And he had every reason to believe it. He had grown up poor and left school with no qualifications. As a 16-year-old, he was jailed for burglary. A life of misery lay ahead of him. Maybe worse. "I could have ended up in a factory," he reflected. "Or ended up dead."

But Ozzy got lucky. He became the singer in a rock band, and the band got famous and rich. A born loser had made good. "Music," he said, "was my salvation."

John Michael Osbourne was born on December 3, 1948, in Aston, Birmingham. He was the fourth of six children, raised in a two-bedroom house. As he later recalled, with typical candour: "We had fuck all."

His dreams of a better life were inspired by hearing the Beatles' Number 1 hit 'She Loves You' on the radio when he was 14. "That's when music took my soul away," he said. "When the Beatles happened, I thought: I'll do that. I'll make a million pounds, get a big house and sit there with a big barrel of beer, just fucking drinking till the end of the day."

After his release from Winson Green prison in 1965, Ozzy took a job at a local auto plant, tuning car horns. He later worked at an abattoir, cleaning away the blood and guts. But at 19, he joined his first rock band, Rare Breed, alongside Geezer Butler. A year later, the pair formed The Polka Tulk Blues Band with Tony Iommi and Bill Ward. And following a brief period as Earth, the band was reinvented as Black Sabbath.

The next 10 years of Ozzy's life were a blur – touring, making records, bingeing on booze and drugs, screwing around, earning and squandering the fortune he had long dreamed of making. He also

Below: Ozzy's crazy antics found a whole new audience with the MTV show *The Osbournes* (2002–05). But he'd been like that for 30 years. "All the trouble I've ever gotten myself into has been attributed to booze and drugs," he has said.

Opposite: By the mid-Eighties, Ozzy was a star in his own right, touring the world and thrilling arena crowds. You wouldn't let this man near your pet doves, though.

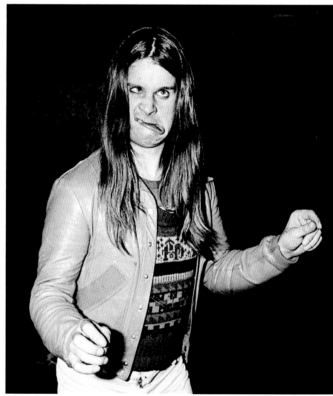

"NO MATTER HOW FUCKED UP I GOT, AS LONG AS I COULD FUNCTION PEOPLE WOULD LIKE IT."

Ozzy Osbourne

got married, to Thelma Mayfair, and started a family. But in 1979 he was fired from Black Sabbath – a consequence of his alcoholism and drug addiction. And in the following decade, he was even more out of control. As he admitted: "All the trouble I've ever gotten myself into has been attributed to booze and drugs."

The chaotic nature of Ozzy's life in the 1980s was encapsulated in a single year: 1982. He had already made headlines in the previous year, when a publicity stunt had gone awry. At a press conference in New York, Ozzy was supposed to release a dove into the air. Instead, in a drunken stupor, he bit the bird's head off – to widespread outrage. In January 1982, during a concert in Des Moines, Iowa, a bat was thrown to Ozzy from the audience. He bit the head off that, too – and was then rushed to hospital for rabies shots. Just four weeks later, Ozzy was arrested in San Antonio, Texas, after he urinated on the Alamo Cenotaph, a sacred monument in American history. He later explained: "I was drunk as a cunt and I needed a piss, so I pissed up the wall."

In the wake of this madness came tragedy: on March 19, Randy Rhoads, Ozzy's guitar player for his solo projects, died in a freak aeroplane crash. Ozzy dealt with his grief in the only way he knew how. July 4, 1982, was when he married for the second time – to his manager Sharon Arden – the ceremony in Maui, Hawaii ended with Ozzy passed out drunk.

Yet he survived it all to become more successful than he had ever been in Black Sabbath. Even his marriage survived – despite his drunken attack on Sharon at their home in Buckinghamshire in 1989, which resulted in Ozzy being arrested for attempted murder. And as he stated in 2013, his love for Sharon, and for their children, was borne out in the hugely popular reality TV series *The Osbournes*. "So many times I heard the same thing," he said. "People told me, 'The language was bad, but we realize that you loved each other.'"

There are many reasons for Ozzy Osbourne to feel that his life has been blessed. He still has his family around him. He has had the good fortune to work in an industry in which a weakness for drugs and alcohol is not only tolerated but is also, to an extent, actively encouraged – something he acknowledged when he said: "No matter how fucked up I got, as long as I could function people would like it."

And in the latter stages of his career, he was granted another wish, when he made an album again with Black Sabbath. As he said in 2013, in all seriousness: "I can honestly say that if I drop dead now, I would die a happy man."

Above and Opposite: Ozzy's onstage persona was a far cry from the more contemplative one of John Osbourne, writer, thinker and occasional animal decapitator.

SABBATH BLOODY SABBATH
(1973)

TONY IOMMI WANTED TO BREAK NEW GROUND WITH SABBATH'S FIFTH
ALBUM. BUT FIRST, HE HAD TO OVERCOME WRITER'S BLOCK. THE GUITARIST
WOULD REDISCOVER HIS MOJO WHEN THE BAND MOVED INTO A CASTLE THAT
WAS BELIEVED TO BE HAUNTED. THE SPOOKY VIBES WOULD INSPIRE AN
ALBUM THAT OZZY WOULD CALL THE GREATEST OF SABBATH'S CAREER.

In June 1973, Black Sabbath were back in Los Angeles to start on their fifth album. It was exactly a year since they had arrived in the city to cut *Vol. 4*, and the set-up was identical. They would live in the same rented mansion in Bel Air, and would record the album at The Record Plant.

It had been a typically busy year. In January the band toured in Australia and New Zealand. In February they set out across Europe. And in March, they were in the UK for a tour that included two dates at The Rainbow theatre in London's Finsbury Park, and ended at Newcastle City Hall.

It was also typical for Sabbath that they pitched up in LA with very little in the way of new songs. And when rehearsals began at the mansion, Iommi was under pressure. The band had always looked to him for their lead. He was the principal songwriter, the source from which so much of Sabbath's music flowed. And nothing was coming.

Compounding the problem was the band's high-rolling lifestyle. Iommi had been happy to return to LA after they'd had such a blast making *Vol. 4*. "We wanted to recreate the experience," he said. Only this time, Iommi felt that the partying had become too much of a distraction. At one point he had to break up a drunken brawl between Ozzy and Geezer – by socking Ozzy on the jaw and knocking him out cold.

In this atmosphere of tension and frustration, Iommi lost focus. "I got writer's block," he recalled to *Classic Rock*. "I just couldn't function." In addition, there was a problem at The Record Plant. The studio room that Sabbath had used for *Vol. 4* was unavailable – much of the space

Left: The cautious Mr Iommi. Look at the concentration and focus in his gaze. You might almost say that he looks "paranoid" in this shot…

Opposite: When the band recorded *Sabbath Bloody Sabbath* at a haunted castle in Gloucestershire, Bill Ward was scared out of his wits, but the location was just the fillip Tony Iommi needed to get his creative juices flowing.

taken up by a huge Moog synthesizer rig specially built for another of The Record Plant's clients, Stevie Wonder.

It was decided that Sabbath should cut their losses and decamp to England. Iommi needed to clear his head in a place that was quiet and secluded – somewhere unlike LA. To that end, a most unusual location was chosen. The band hired Clearwell Castle in Gloucestershire, an imposing, mock Gothic pile built in 1728.

From the moment they arrived, Iommi felt that the place was "creepy". And when he and Geezer explored the castle one day, they had a strange and unsettling experience. As they reached a long corridor in the basement leading to the dungeons, the two men saw a figure in black entering a doorway. They followed it into the armoury, a room with swords and shields on the walls and weapons arranged on a table. But there was no trace of the figure in black. And there was no other exit from the room. "Bloody hell," Iommi said to Butler. "This is weird!"

Later, when Iommi spoke to the owner of the castle, she said in a casual manner that what they had seen was a ghost. She also told Bill Ward a story about the room he had chosen as his bedroom – that it was haunted by the spirit of a maid who had committed suicide by jumping from the window. Ward was so scared that he went to bed each night with a knife beside him.

Opposite: *A New Musical Express* press advert from March 10, 1973, promoting Black Sabbath's UK tour and their growing album back catalogue.

Above and Top Right: Ozzy and Bill, iconic in very different ways; the former an extrovert who sang in a monotone, the latter an introvert who played like a man possessed.

Right: Geezer Butler is the creative force behind Sabbath's lyrics – as well as a bass player of phenomenal talent and panache.

"IT WAS THE GOLDEN PERIOD,
THE PINNACLE OF SABBATH."

Ozzy Osbourne

But for Iommi, the sinister atmosphere at Clearwell Castle had the desired effect. It inspired him to write the menacing riff for what would become the title track of the new album, *Sabbath Bloody Sabbath*. And with that, his writer's block lifted. More songs quickly followed, and in September the band recorded the album at Morgan Studios in Willesden, north London.

The result was the band's most ambitious album to date. The title track was as heavy as any of their early classics – featuring not one but two of Iommi's greatest riffs. And across the whole album there was an experimental approach. Ozzy composed the song 'Who Are You' on a Moog – touché, Stevie! A string section was utilized on the brilliant, mesmerizing final track 'Spiral Architect'. And on 'Sabbra Cadabra', there was a guest performance by Rick Wakeman of Yes on piano. Wakeman had befriended Sabbath when Yes toured with them in '72. For his contribution to 'Sabbra Cadabra', he declined payment and was instead rewarded in beer.

Produced by the band and released on December 1, 1973, *Sabbath Bloody Sabbath* hit Number 4 in the UK and Number 11 in the US. A review of the album in *Rolling Stone* hailed Sabbath as a band completely in tune with the zeitgeist: "Call it the blues of the decade, or heavy metal – whatever the name for their music, Black Sabbath are a true 70s band." And as Ozzy later said: "The golden period of Sabbath was *Master Of Reality, Vol. 4* and then, right at the pinnacle, *Sabbath Bloody Sabbath*."

Above: In the 1970s, the small- to medium-sized venue circuit was essential for even the biggest bands – a far cry from today's Academy and arena trek.

Opposite: The off-duty Osbourne as a young star in his prime – but how much of his wealth was real, and how much was simply management-created smoke and mirrors?

SABBATH BLOODY SABBATH

This was the song that smashed Iommi's writer's block as the group reassembled in the Welsh castle. "I just started this riff," he said, "and then they started up, and it worked well."

Allegedly named after a headline in the late, lamented British music weekly *Melody Maker*, it is quintessential Sabbath, a detuned, riffing dirge whose fearsome weight lifts only slightly to create contrasting moments. It blew the cobwebs away from around the band and the dark corners of their dungeon, giving rise to a new outpouring of ideas.

Said Ozzy: "The title track was something about the word 'God' and changing it all around. Instead of 'God bless all of you,' it was 'Bog Blast all of you.' Geezer Butler wrote those words and he was very fucking stoned. He must have been."

Sabbath analysts have suggested that Geezer's lyrics betray a weariness and a suspicion of the phenomenon surrounding Black Sabbath – an opinion backed by Bill Ward. Geezer wrote: "Dreams turn to nightmares, heaven turns to hell/Burned out confusion, nothing more to tell."

The bass player, however, has reported especially happy memories of making the album. Talking to writer John Stix in 1994 with Tony Iommi, he said: "Right before that, we were in a terrible slump. We were all exhausted from touring. We weren't getting on very well. Then Tony came up with the riff for *Sabbath Bloody Sabbath* and everybody sparked into life. The year while we were doing that was a really good year, personally. I'll always remember that album and look back on it with a good feeling."

Indeed, he stated that of all of the Ozzy-era albums, it was the one he would urge fans to rediscover, citing the title track as a personal favourite. "It was a whole new era for us," continued Geezer. "We felt really open on that album. It was a great atmosphere, good time, great coke! Just like a new birth for me."

Tony Iommi agreed: "Some great tracks on that album. It was a great feeling from rehearsals to writing to recording. It was just a great time. That was a good album for me. I enjoyed that."

Opposite: Taking the world by storm, stage by stage, with Ozzy on truly flamboyant form. If you can't hit the high notes, at least look the part.

Below: The moustache-less Tony Iommi was barely recognizable at this early point in Sabbath's careers. That soon changed…

A NATIONAL ACROBAT

"That was just me thinking about who selects what sperm gets through the egg," explained Geezer Butler, off-handedly.

And it's just as well he did, because no one else would have guessed it. "When little worlds collide/I'm trapped inside my embryonic cell," sang Ozzy, broadcasting Geezer's mysterious allusions to the wriggling failures and the unborn child that was never conceived.

From there on in, there's lots of talk about the seeds, the secret, the soul and the life beyond. It would appear that the text deliberately widens to represent something bigger, something human, to urge the audience to make the most of their time on earth, and to state a belief in survival, in some form, beyond death.

There again, Geezer may simply have decided in a moment of madness that sperm have souls, that they might be reincarnated along with everyone else or welcomed into the eternal kingdoms of heaven and hell.

Fans applauded "A National Acrobat", dwelling on its diverse musical power and Iommi's affecting guitar riff, although one reviewer appealed: "The subject matter of the song is not quite clear to me. Does anyone know?" And another ventured: "I get the idea that this song is about someone who has seen the world and knows all that life has to offer."

WHO ARE YOU?

Not even distantly related to The Who track of the same name, this was the first real song that Ozzy ever wrote. It's the album's big synthesizer track, and one which has stood the test of time very badly as far as Sabbath fans are concerned.

Quoted by Steven Rosen, Ozzy had this to say: "I dig singing the spacey things with electronics. I dig this emptiness thing. The synthesizer gives this empty feeling of depth and distance. It's like forever.

"Like "Who Are You?" I wrote that in the kitchen while my wife was cooking some food. I had a synthesizer on the table and I was just fucking about with a tape machine and it just came out...

"I never played instruments. I don't even know what the fuck I played. I really don't know what key or chord or what notes I played. It's just the sound."

"Please, I beg you, tell me, in the name of hell, who are you? Who are you?" implores Ozzy as the song reaches its conclusion.

Determinedly non-musical in his new capacity as a writer, Ozzy was nevertheless lambasted, not so much for his nasal vocals but for his very nerve in allowing his firstborn song to be interpreted and accompanied by a machine.

"We were never afraid to do whatever we felt at the time," replied Geezer Butler. "I think that's what kept us as Black Sabbath. Listen to anything past the first three albums – we do soul stuff, not what everybody else would do, but there's funky bass lines in there or funky guitar bits, some synthesizers, and straight-ahead ballads ("Changes"). Anything. We felt it would kill the band if we weren't allowed to grow up within it."

Tony Iommi enthused: "Rick Wakeman, who played on "Who Are You?", was great, really great. He was wild back then. We took Yes on tour with us, and brought them to America on their first tour. But Rick used to travel with us and not Yes for some reason."

SPIRAL ARCHITECT

Ozzy Osbourne thinks of Geezer Butler when he thinks of "Spiral Architect".

"Geezer's an incredible lyricist," said Ozzy. "Not many people know he wrote 90 per cent (Butler would say 95 per cent) of the lyrics for Sabbath. I'll never forget when he wrote the lyrics to "Spiral Architect". I was on the phone and I asked him if he had the lyrics for me to sing yet.

"He says to me, 'Got a pen?' He started off, 'Sorcerers of madness, selling me their time...' And I go, 'You're fucking reading this out of a book. You're joking!' My mouth dropped open." Geezer, clearly still fascinated by human creation, explained: "It was about life's experiences being added to a person's DNA to create a unique individual."

At its close, the song decides, optimistically, "Of all the things I value most of all/I look upon my earth and feel the warmth/And know that it is good." Sabbath were gradually changing their tune, reaching for the positive while recognizing and documenting the opposite forces.

"Spiral Architect", described by one critic as a "philosophical symphony", remains one of the album's stand-out tracks with its ambitious but confident electric/acoustic combinations, keyboards and string effects.

Other tracks on the album are "Fluff", a much maligned, sluggish and layered instrumental deemed too long for its own good; "Sabbra Cadabra", a shag-happy slice of rock'n'roll adorned by keyboards; the highly rated and grungy "Killing Yourself To Live", with its building tempos and guitar solo; and the sturdy "Looking For Today", which is carried up to the very edges of pop melody by a repeating riff augmented by handclaps, keyboards and a flute arrangement.

Above: The angel and the devil at close quarters on stage – but which was which? All these years later, it's still hard to tell the difference.

Opposite: Peace signs in full effect and rock-star garb present and correct, Ozzy Osbourne appears here as perhaps the perfect 1970s stage singer.

SABOTAGE
(1975)

IN 1974, THE FOUR MEMBERS OF BLACK SABBATH DECIDED TO FIRE
THEIR MANAGER IN A DISPUTE OVER MONEY. THE RESULT WAS A
LONG AND BITTER LEGAL STRUGGLE THAT WOULD THREATEN TO
END THE BAND'S CAREER, A STRUGGLE THAT WOULD INSPIRE THE
BLEAKLY IRONIC TITLE OF THEIR SIXTH ALBUM: *SABOTAGE*.

It was a day that Ozzy Osbourne, Tony Iommi, Geezer Butler and Bill Ward would never forget. On April 6, 1974, Black Sabbath played at the California Jam festival at the Ontario Motor Speedway racetrack, 56 km (35 miles) from Los Angeles. It was an event co-headlined by two other superstar British rock acts, Emerson, Lake & Palmer and Deep Purple. The size of the audience was estimated at between 250,000 and 350,000. And when Sabbath took to the stage in late afternoon sunshine – with Ozzy yelling, "Let's have a party!" – it was the cue for mass hysteria.

In that moment, it seemed that Black Sabbath were on top of the world. And yet, behind the scenes, this was a band in turmoil. Physically and mentally, they were exhausted. As Butler said: "We hadn't stopped touring and recording for five years." Worse, they were short of cash. They had all bought country houses and flashy cars – the usual rock star trappings. But for all of the band's success, they did not feel rich. "We never had more than a grand in the bank," Butler claimed. "Any time we needed money, we had to ask the manager, Patrick Meehan, to send us some." The mood within the band had turned mutinous. After Sabbath returned to England from the California Jam, they notified Meehan of their intention to end their contract with his company Worldwide Artists.

This would not come easily, or cheaply. The battle between Black Sabbath and Patrick Meehan would endure for the greater part of a year as the band laboured over their sixth album. "We were trying to write and record the album while trying to leave Meehan," Butler said. "We spent most of the time in lawyers' offices, and were being served writs while we were in the studio."

But in a time of adversity, Sabbath pulled together. "We all relied on each other," Butler recalled to *Classic Rock*. "There was no-one

Left: Black Sabbath at their manic best, performing in London in 1974.

Opposite: Ozzy Osbourne performing live in Copenhagen, Denmark, on January 11, 1974.

MARQUEE·MARTIN AGENCY LTD 41-43 WARDOUR STREET LONDON W I TEL:01.734-7464

Directors   J. Martin (managing)   J. G. A. Toogood   D. C. Barber   S. G. White
Licensed Annually by the City of Westminster

021 454 7020
JM SIMPSON.

co'd/js

An Agreement

made the....8th....day of....June............19..70.

Between............Lionel Digby...hereinafter referred to as the "Management"
of the one part and......Black Sabbath...hereinafter referred to as the "Artiste"
of the other part.

Witnesseth

that the Management hereby engages the Artiste and the Artiste accepts an

engagement to { present......Black Sabbath..

appear as ....known..

(or in his usual entertainment) at the Dance Hall/Theatre or other Venue and from the dates and for the
periods and at the salary stated in the Schedule hereto.

SCHEDULE

The Artiste agrees to appear at....1............Evening and.........—........Matinee performances

at a salary of { £...200.0.0d................................
............% of the gross advance and door takings. The Management guarantees a minimum
of £......................

...1...day(s) at....Town Hall,.................................... on......1st July 1970.............
.........day(s) at....Torquay.. on...
.........day(s) at.. on...

SPECIAL STIPULATIONS

I. The Artiste shall not, without the written consent of the Management, appear at any public place of entertainment within
a radius of.................miles of the venue during a period of....................weeks immediately prior to and....................
weeks immediately following the engagement.

2. The Management shall, at their own expense, provide (a) first-class Amplification and Microphone equipment (b) Grand
Piano and (c) (at dances only) Relief Band or music.
The Management agrees that any other bands performing the engagement(s) shall be composed of members of the Musicians'
Union, and in the event of Musicians' Union action arising from the engagement of non-Unionists, the Management will be
responsible for payment of the full fees as stated in the agreement; also that the playing of Recorded music shall not exceed
Twenty minutes during the performance.

3. The price of admission to be not less than....................per person in advance and....................at the door.

4. The Orchestra/Band shall play for a maximum of:....1........hours in separate sessions Dance to commence at....................
and terminate at................. Approximate playing times for Artiste, ...to....................and....................
to...................

5. Salary payable by................cash to the Artistes on the night..
....

6. The Artiste shall supply, without charge, photographs, wording for publicity and programme details (when required) to
....for receipt not later than........................days before the commencement of the
engagement.

7. ....Black Sabbath..................................shall appear personally throughout the performance.

8. Arrival time ....7.00 p.m.

This Agency is not responsible for any non-fulfilment of

Contracts by Proprietors, Managers or Artistes but

every reasonable safeguard is assured.

Signature ...

Address ....

....

else we could trust. We were constantly stoned, so we were never confrontational towards each other. It was an 'us-against-them' attitude in the band."

The making of *Sabotage* was not all trouble and strife. While recording at Morgan Studios, where they had cut *Sabbath Bloody Sabbath*, the band made full use of the house bar and its dartboard – which they christened "Bill's beard" due to the fraying strands of cork around the number three. Butler also recalled spending an entire evening playing darts in the bar with the Rolling Stones' drummer Charlie Watts.

But Iommi admitted that the ongoing litigation had a subliminal effect on the album. "With *Sabotage*, the sound was a bit harder than *Sabbath Bloody Sabbath*," he said. "That was brought on by all the aggravation we felt." This hard sound is most evident on the album's bludgeoning first track 'Hole In The Sky', and on 'Symptom Of The Universe', one of the heaviest and most influential songs that Sabbath ever recorded – in Iommi's words, "very fast and very loud."

There is also a track that's even spookier than the song 'Black Sabbath'. Described by Ward as "a demonic chant", 'Supertzar' features the English Chamber Choir singing over a death-march riff, with tubular bells carrying an echo of the supernatural horror film *The Exorcist*. "As we mixed that track," Ward said, "I thought, my God, this is incredible! It was somewhat revolutionary." Ozzy called it "a noise like God conducting the soundtrack to the end of the world."

And with the song they chose to end the album, Sabbath made a thinly veiled attack on Patrick Meehan. As Ward explained: "Geezer was able to take all our feelings about what had happened – mine, Ozzy's and Tony's – and put it all down. We were like, 'Yeah – you gave it to him!' Geezer was our legal defendant on that song." It was named, aptly, 'The Writ'.

Sabotage was released on June 27, 1975. In the UK it was business as usual: another Top 10 hit. In the US, less so: it peaked at Number 28. But the album had mostly positive reviews. *Rolling Stone* stated: "*Sabotage* is not only Black Sabbath's best record since *Paranoid*, it might be their best ever." And by the end of the year, the band was rid, at last, of Patrick Meehan.

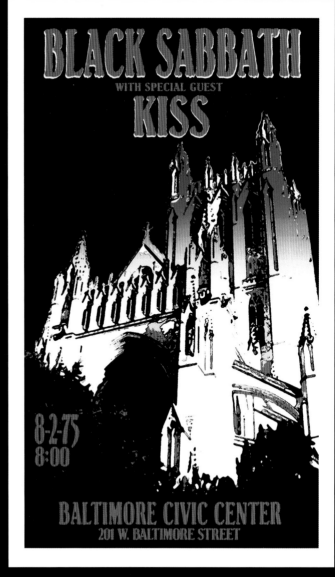

For Ozzy, this would be an album best forgotten. "I can't listen to *Sabotage*," he said, "because all I think of is everything going wrong at the time." He even hated the album cover, and what he described as his "homo in a kimono" look. But for Sabbath connoisseurs, *Sabotage* would come to be regarded as the band's lost classic: the last great album of the original Ozzy era. And Bill Ward agrees. As he told *Classic Rock* in 2012: "That album was so hard for us to make. But when I listen back to it now... God, it's incredible."

Opposite: An early Black Sabbath appearance contract from 1970. For a fee of £200 (to be paid in cash on the night) the band were contracted to perform for the Marquee Club event at Torquay Town Hall.

Left: Black Sabbath in rehearsals in 1974. Around this time they started to question whether there was any point to the endless recording and touring, "just to pay the lawyers".

Above: A poster of Black Sabbath's concert at the Baltimore Civic Center, Maryland, August 2, 1975. Legendary US rock band Kiss provided the support.

HOLE IN THE SKY/
SYMPTOM OF THE UNIVERSE

Blasting the album into life, "Hole In The Sky" and "Symptom Of the Universe" together announced that Sabbath were back in business. The headbanging "Hole In The Sky" – once memorably described as "music to demolish buildings by" – was deliberately chosen as the first track because of its barbarously simple rock formula: no keyboards, no flights of fancy. It was a statement of intent.

On Geezer Butler's part, it was a statement of something else. And, no, he wasn't prophesying any problems with the ozone layer. According to Tony Iommi, Geezer's lyrics dwelled on "sort of a universal thing. It's basically about the astral plane."

Taking the chance to cock a snook at the "dogs of war" – arguably a reference to the hated "war pigs" – and again an attack on the greed and affluence of the West, Geezer turned in a typically spacey lyric in which he was "seeing nowhere through the eyes of a lie".

In the most gloriously incomprehensible couplet, he confides: "The synonyms of all the things that I've said/Are just the riddles that are built in my head."

Linking "Hole In The Sky" to "Symptom Of The Universe" is the 49-second, acoustic guitar snippet, "Don't Start (Too Late)". Tony Iommi told Steven Rosen: "The way we came about that was the engineer was a comical chap and he kept saying, 'Don't start! Don't start!' But it was too late, because we had started."

Shattering these fragile moments, Sabbath storm back loud and proud, Ozzy screaming like the banshee of his reputation and Iommi knocking out another of his killer riffs, with "Symptom Of The Universe". A lengthy track, it plunges dramatically from the savage attack of its first few minutes to a laid-back and jazzy conclusion with Iommi on acoustic guitar.

Journeying again through time and space, the lyrics pour out theories about love, rebirth, eternity and the universe, ending on a brightly optimistic note: "We'll find happiness together in the summer skies of love".

MEGALOMANIA

Considered by many Sabbath fans to be both the centrepiece and the masterpiece of *Sabotage*, the unsettling "Megalomania" checks in at almost 10 minutes.

It builds theatrically, compellingly, from a starting-gate of subtle, acoustic restraint into a riot of multi-riffing guitar that bangs out rounds of hostile fire and feedback as Ozzy rises up to denounce the god who had for so long imprisoned and persecuted Geezer Butler, or the character he had created.

Once asked to explain the song, Tony Iommi confessed to being no more qualified than anybody else to decipher the lyrics. "It's hard to quite explain that number,' he chuckled. 'Geezer wrote the words...'"

Below: The madman in Ozzy came out on stage, and at least in this period of Sabbath's career, off stage as well. But don't we want that in a rock star?

Opposite: Geezer playing a custom eight-string bass made for him for master luthier John Birch. Note the classical guitar-style fingerpicking he's using.

Whether it was the Biblical God, the god of darkness or even the god of success, desire, love or cocaine, its hold was something that Geezer's hero "could not control". The words describe a life of shame and sorrow, in which the protagonist emerges from the shadows to square up to some hefty, personal demon, at the same time fighting schizophrenia and the knowledge that he was liable to slip at any moment.

"I've seized my soul in the fires of hell/Peace of mind eluded me, but now it's all mine," wails Ozzy, intermittently urging the tormenting power, "Why don't you just get out of my life, yeah?"

Ozzy commented at the time about the general nature of Sabbath lyrics: "They're not downer lyrics, they're just telling everybody where it's at. That's all it is. People must think we sleep off rafters with wings on our backs every night, taking reds and drinking wine. We see a lot and we write about what we see...

"Love wouldn't go with the style of music we play. It would be like going to see *Frankenstein* with the *Sound Of Music* soundtrack behind it."

SUPERTZAR

Although *Sabotage* is primarily an all-out, hard rock album, written to be played live onstage, it does have its moments of light relief and diversion – memorably with the instrumental "Supertzar".

Here, Black Sabbath were joined by the full English Chamber Choir, arranged by Will Malone, who provided an unearthly counterbalance to Iommi's dedicated riffing. Indeed, there are those who feel that the idea could have stretched to create a full-blown, operatic, metal anthem.

Iommi recently stated: "It was a thing we said years ago when we did "Laguna Sunrise" and "Supertzar" with the choir – we went out to do what we liked. We played what we enjoyed."

"It sounds like one of those epic, bloody *Ben Hur* themes," countered Ozzy.

He later claimed: "I remember being stuck in Miami with no dough during this album. We called the label to get more money and they sent us a telegram saying, 'Don't worry – the hamburgers are on the way." Sick fucking joke. It wasn't a happy time, although when Tony came up with the riff to "Supertzar", it fucking pinned my ears back. I was *gobsmacked*."

AM I GOING INSANE (RADIO)

Described by Tony Iommi as "a sort of Moog [synthesizer] guitar groove", this was clearly an emotional exercise for its author, Ozzy. He revealed in 1976: "Doing "Am I Going Insane" exorcised the feelings in me. I don't think I'm going mad any more, but I'm still angry – I've *always* been angry."

Eerie atmospheres compounded a lyric which talks, with fabulous déjà vu, of being paranoid and of being a "schizo brain". Seemingly, it encapsulated Ozzy's anxieties about his place in the world, and the fears that assailed him about staying in Sabbath and, also, about leaving them. Oh, and in case the bracketed "Radio" implies that there may be another edit – there isn't. 'Radio' was rhyming slang for 'radio rental', or 'mental'.

THE WRIT

This was the big, autobiographical moment; the group's eight-minute tirade against the music industry and its inherent ruthlessness. Spilling out all of the anger, dismay, defiance and bloodlust that they had felt during their management struggles and their enforced retreat into an unanswerable legal quagmire, Black Sabbath were finally able to put the gloves on and retaliate.

"What kind of people do you think we are?" challenges Ozzy, as the track courses through its riff-riven changes. "Another joker who's a rock and roll star for you, just for you?"

Charged up with all the righteous fury of men with the moral high ground, individuals who had worked for and believed in the honour of rock'n'roll only to be repaid with lies, false promises and betrayal, Sabbath warn that they have transformed their hatred into a curse before eventually looking forward to a time when "everything is gonna work out fine".

It's probably the most direct lyric in their repertoire, and all the more chilling for it. Forget old red-eye crouching over there in the corner of your darkest nightmare: this is about real life and real people – the nightmare in your living room. "The Writ" is recommended listening for every would-be musician.

Other tracks on the album are "The Thrill Of It All", addressing "Mr Jesus" with feedback, moodswings and an unusual tendency to prog-rock, and the 23-second "Blow On A Jug", included on some original vinyl and cassette album copies. It was an informal and low-volume recording of Ozzy and Bill Ward larking about in the studio, à la Nitty Gritty Dirt Band, tacked onto the end of "The Writ" – the calm after the storm.

Opposite: "You see, we come from Aston…" You could sit and have a fairly relaxed chat with Ozzy at times like this, when he wasn't in the grip of some substance or other.

Below: Geezer and Ozzy seized by the adrenaline of the moment; Iommi calm and collected, as ever, keeping the train on the rails.

Next spread: Rolling through America in the mid-Seventies, Black Sabbath took their message of hyperactive devilry to the masses… and they loved it.

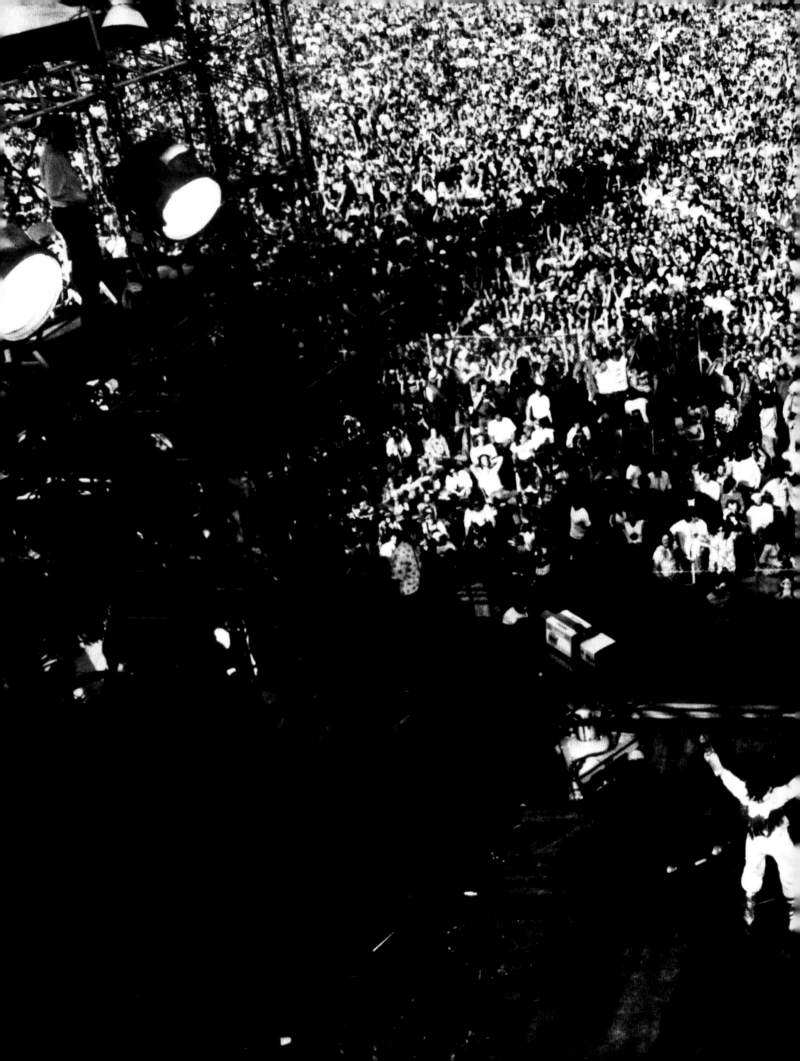

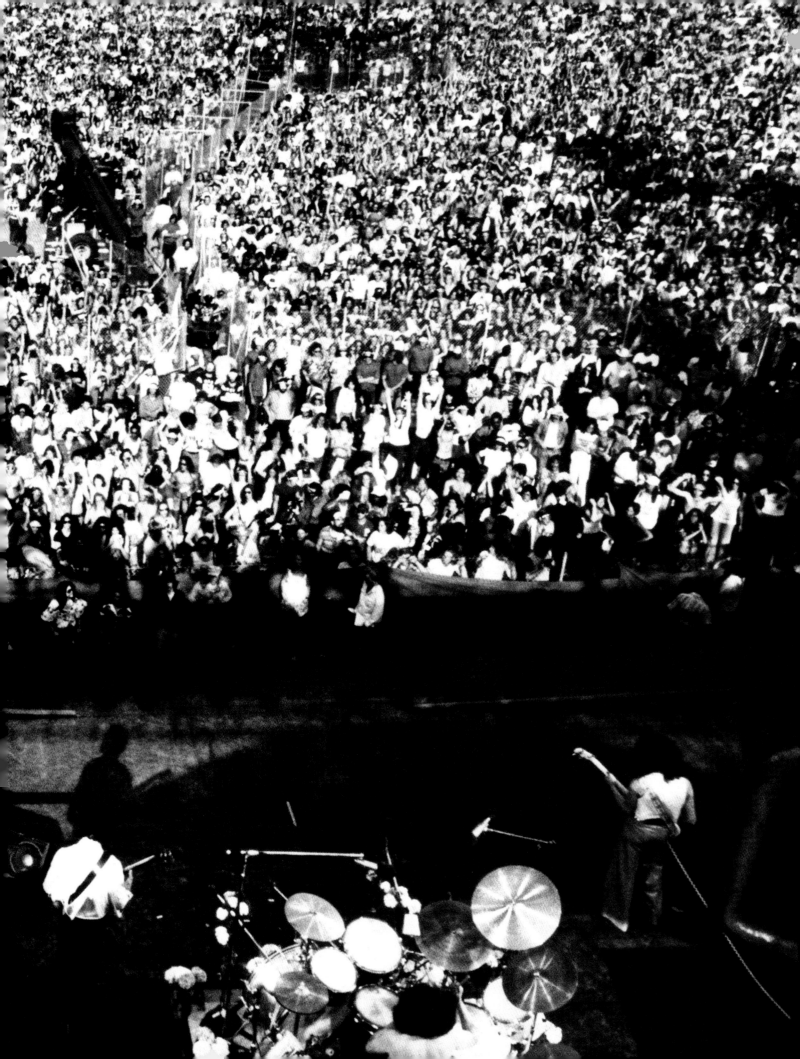

PROFILE
GEEZER BUTLER

HIS WIFE GLORIA CALLS HIM TERRY. TO MILLIONS OF BLACK SABBATH
FANS, HE IS KNOWN AS GEEZER. TONY IOMMI DESCRIBES HIM AS
"THE BEST BASS PLAYER IN ROCK". OZZY CALLS HIM A "FUCKING
UNBELIEVABLE LYRICIST". AND GEEZER BUTLER'S TALENTS DO NOT END
THERE. "I'M A GOOD VEGAN COOK," HE SAID. "THROUGH NECESSITY."

Ozzy Osbourne has a funny way of explaining how he interprets the lyrics that Geezer Butler has written for Black Sabbath's songs. "Geezer is the science fiction guy in the band," Ozzy said. "He comes up with all these words that I don't understand. And I transform them from his brain to my mouth."

For the greater part of Sabbath's career, Butler has been the band's primary lyric writer, on landmark songs such as 'War Pigs', 'Paranoid', 'Iron Man', 'Children Of The Grave' and 'Symptom Of The Universe' – and the defining track on the band's 13 album, 'God Is Dead?'.

It was by default that Butler became Sabbath's lyricist. "Ozzy tried but became bored quickly," he said. "After that it became my job." And it was a role in which he excelled. On the early Sabbath albums, Butler's words became as integral to the band's identity as his fluid and inventive bass playing.

Born on July 17, 1949 in Aston, Terence Michael Joseph Butler was the product of an Irish Catholic family. "I was very religious growing up," he said. "So I knew The Bible backwards, and in Latin." As a child he loved to read and to write stories. He also earned his nickname while still at school. "I used to call everyone 'geezer'," he explained. "So eventually everybody started calling me 'Geezer'."

He started out as a guitarist, influenced by the Beatles and, in particular, John Lennon. It was as rhythm guitarist that he joined his first band, Rare Breed, in 1967. He knew of Ozzy before then, although he kept his distance. "Ozzy was a skinhead," he recalled, "and I had hair down to my waist. We wouldn't speak. In fact, we wouldn't even walk on the same side of the road." When Ozzy auditioned for Rare Breed, Butler quickly realized that he was an unusual character: "Mental." But they grew to like each other. They stuck together to become founding members of Black Sabbath. And as Butler said in an interview with *Classic Rock*, he feels that he and Ozzy were destined to achieve great things together. "I definitely think that everything is fated, or at least some of it is," he said. "You can't explain why this band got together. It just happened out of the blue, as if it was all meant to happen. It's weird."

It was Butler who gave the title to their first and defining song, 'Black Sabbath'. It was also his idea to take this as the name of the band. He had a fascination with the occult. "I was into all the magic stuff," he recalled. "Dennis Wheatley, Aleister Crowley." The Satanic imagery in the lyrics to the song 'Black Sabbath', written by Ozzy and Bill Ward, was echoed in what Butler wrote for another track on Sabbath's debut album, 'N.I.B.'. The difference was that Butler's writing was more nuanced. "'N.I.B.' was about the Devil falling in love and totally changing, becoming a good person," he said.

Butler would develop over the years as one of the most original and thought-provoking writers in rock 'n' roll. "As long as I didn't write typical clichéd lyrics, I was happy," he said. "I also tried to write from experience. 'Paranoid' came from the depression I was cursed with, so I was more familiar with that word than the rest of the band. And really, I was a bit of a 'peace and love, man' bloke. Growing up in Aston, I'd had my share of violence and negativity, so I usually tried to instill some hope into the bleaker images of my lyrics."

Away from Black Sabbath, Butler has always been a private man. He said in 2013 that he is happiest at his home in Los Angeles with just his wife and their six dogs and seven cats for company. An avowed supporter of animal rights, he has been a vegan since 1980.

Butler's greatest regret is the sacking of Ozzy from Black Sabbath in 1979. "Before that," he said, "none of us had ever imagined not being in the band." For this reason, he said that he could never again listen to the album that preceded Ozzy's exit, *Never Say Die!*. "That album brings back such horrible memories," he explained.

He also expressed his regret that Bill Ward was not involved in the *13* album. For so many years, he and Ward had their own unique chemistry as the engine room in Black Sabbath – one that Butler could never hope to replicate with a different drummer.

Nonetheless, he reckoned that what Sabbath achieved with this album would be a fitting end to their career. "This is the perfect way to finish," he said. "If this is the last thing we ever do – fine."

And with this, Geezer Butler said that he would happily retire. He stated simply: "We've completed what we were put on Earth to do."

Opposite: Terry 'Geezer' Butler: a man who ultimately conquered his demons, embraced a vegan lifestyle and found his role somewhere in the middle of the most crazed band on earth.

"AS LONG AS I DIDN'T WRITE TYPICAL CLICHÉD LYRICS, I WAS HAPPY."

Geezer Butler

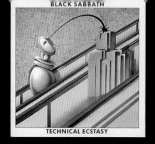

TECHNICAL ECSTASY
(1976)

AFTER *SABOTAGE*, AN ALBUM MADE AMID CIRCUMSTANCES THAT
GEEZER BUTLER DESCRIBED AS "TOTAL CHAOS", BLACK SABBATH WOULD
NEVER BE THE SAME AGAIN. FURTHER CHAOS ENSUED WHEN THE BAND
MISGUIDEDLY ATTEMPTED TO MANAGE THEIR BUSINESS THEMSELVES.
AND THEIR NEXT ALBUM *TECHNICAL ECSTASY* HAD AN EXPERIMENTAL
SOUND THAT WOULD ALIENATE MANY DIE-HARD SABBATH FANS.

The long and traumatic legal battle that overshadowed the recording of *Sabotage* had taken a lot out of Black Sabbath. "It changed us," Bill Ward said. "I have no doubts about that."

This much became evident immediately after the band's split from manager Patrick Meehan was finalized. With Meehan out of the frame, the members of Black Sabbath decided that they would manage the band's affairs themselves. It was a bad idea. The four of them had been under immense stress while making *Sabotage*. They had lost a lot of money during litigation. They were frazzled from touring, boozing and drugs. And without a designated manager to mediate between them, the arguments escalated. "The band was disintegrating," Geezer Butler told *Classic Rock*. "It was a very big strain on us."

Matters came to a head when the band toured the UK in October 1975. "I really wasn't looking forward to going out on the road again

and managing ourselves," Butler said. "It was on that tour when things started going pear-shaped. We quickly realized that proper management required professional organization."

In early 1976, Don Arden was announced as the manager of Black Sabbath. The self-styled "Mr. Big" of rock 'n' roll managers, Arden had first courted Sabbath back in 1970 – behind the back of then manager Jim Simpson. In the 60s, Arden had made a success of the Small Faces. He also had a fearsome reputation, which is why Sabbath had turned him down in 1970. As Osbourne said: "We heard stories about him dangling people out of his office window and stubbing cigars out on people's foreheads." Six years later, Sabbath decided that this ballbreaker was their best option. "We knew Don Arden," Butler explained. "So we thought, better the devil you know."

Arden was not the only new face in the Sabbath camp. On the Sabotage tour, the band had enlisted a keyboard player, Birmingham-based Gerald "Jezz" Woodroffe. Until that point, Sabbath had always performed as a quartet, but Woodroffe had been brought in so that the band could better reproduce the more complex material from *Sabotage* and *Sabbath Bloody Sabbath*. When Iommi started writing songs for the next album, Woodroffe worked with him as a sounding board for Iommi's ideas. And although Woodroffe was not a co-writer – in Sabbath, songwriting was a closed shop – he would play a prominent role in the recording of the album.

In June 1976, after six weeks of writing and rehearsing in England, Sabbath flew to Miami to record at Criteria Studios, where Eric Clapton had cut his Number 1 album *461 Ocean Boulevard*, and the Bee Gees had made their disco-influenced comeback *Main Course* – an album with artwork by Drew Struzan, creator of the demonic image on the cover of *Sabbath Bloody Sabbath*. In the studio room adjacent to Sabbath's, the Eagles were recording what would become one of the biggest selling albums of all time, *Hotel California*. And at various times, the Eagles had to stop work because Sabbath were playing so loud that the noise was leaking through the walls.

What emerged from these sessions was a new and different Sabbath sound. Keyboards, played by Woodroffe, were featured on every track – even the heaviest songs such as 'Back Street Kids' and 'Dirty Women', the latter inspired by the prostitutes that Butler had observed around Miami. One song, 'Rock 'N' Roll Doctor', was a hard rock boogie with a clunking cowbell – it could have passed for a song by Kiss. And there

Opposite: The four horsemen of the apocalypse, ready to rock. Geezer looks particularly energised; what can he have been taking backstage?

Above: Black Sabbath during a Madison Square Garden show in 1976. *Technical Ecstasy* was not a great commercial success stateside. It finally went gold in the US in 1997.

were two bands. *She's Gone*, sung by Ozzy, and *It's Alright*, written and sung by Ward in the style of John Lennon. "At that time I was writing a lot of softer music," Ward said. "I was playing this stuff at home, in a different head space. It was very relaxing. When you play drums in a band like Black Sabbath, driving the band, you need to have a different head space when you come home."

The album, *Technical Ecstasy*, was released on September 25, 1976, with a cover by Hipgnosis, the design company whose iconic album covers included Pink Floyd's *The Dark Side Of The Moon* and Led Zeppelin's *Houses Of The Holy*. Storm Thorgerson of Hipgnosis described the image for *Technical Ecstasy* as "some sort of mechanic copulation."

A review of the album in British rock weekly *Melody Maker* praised the band's ability to "break the mould and still provide exciting music". But many Sabbath fans disagreed. Sales of *Technical Ecstasy* were slow. It was the first Sabbath album to peak outside the UK Top 10, and in the US it stalled outside the Top 50. According to Iommi: "That was when the decline really started."

Left: Bill Ward, approaching the end of his peak as a drummer; within three years of the '77 dates, his alcoholism would have rendered him unable to tour.

Below: Black Sabbath toured in 1976/77, promoting their seventh studio album *Technical Ecstasy*. They were supported by Nutz for their March 6, 1977 appearance at the New Bingley Hall, Stafford.

Opposite: Tony Iommi, regal as always – despite a very real sense that the new punk rock movement might soon make his music obsolete.

Harvey Goldsmith Entertainments
presents

BLACK SABBATH

in concert

SUNDAY 6th MARCH 1977

at 7.30 pm Doors open 6.45 pm

Tickets £2.00 inc. VAT

New Bingley Hall, Stafford

No re-admission
for conditions see reverse
to be retained and produced
on demand.

Scot. Auto. Edin.

Nº 6080

Purchase of this ticket signifies agreement to the following:

The right to refuse admission is reserved.

The right to alter the composition of the programme is reserved.

Tickets cannot be exchanged or money refunded for any reason whatsoever including cancellation of the concert or part of it.

Ticket holders consent to the filming and sound recording of themselves as members of the audience.

No bottles will be allowed inside the hall.

WARNING: Do not be misled by unofficial sellers of "Souvenirs" and "Programmes" outside the hall.

"THE BAND WAS DISINTEGRATING.
IT WAS A VERY BIG STRAIN ON US."

Geezer Butler

NEVER SAY DIE!
(1978)

ON NOVEMBER 5, 1977, BLACK SABBATH MADE THE SHOCK ANNOUNCEMENT THAT OZZY OSBOURNE HAD LEFT THE BAND. JUST TWO MONTHS LATER, AFTER SABBATH TRIED OUT A NEW SINGER, OZZY WAS BACK WITH THEM AND RECORDING A NEW ALBUM, *NEVER SAY DIE!*. AND THAT WAS WHEN THINGS TURNED REALLY UGLY…

When Black Sabbath replaced Ozzy Osbourne with Dave Walker on November 26, 1977, it was an act of desperation. This much was evident in the only public appearance that Walker made with Sabbath – on the Midlands TV show *Look! Hear!* on January 6, 1978. Walker had a strong voice, but he couldn't sing 'War Pigs' like Ozzy. Nobody could.

Tony Iommi brought Walker into the band because he had no other choice. For Sabbath to continue, they needed a singer. And as he later admitted, Iommi always believed that Ozzy would come back. It just happened quicker than he expected. Only three weeks after Sabbath's TV performance with Walker came the news that Ozzy had rejoined the band.

It was, however, a false dawn. Ozzy's return solved one problem but created many more. The band would be stretched to breaking point during the making of *Never Say Die!*. And as Ozzy later said: "That album was the end of the beginning."

The problems began as soon as Ozzy heard the new songs that the band had been working on during his brief absence. Some had been written and demoed with Dave Walker. Ozzy liked only one of these songs, 'Junior's Eyes'. The rest, he dismissed out of hand. It meant that Iommi would have to write almost an entire album from scratch – a situation exacerbated by the fact that a studio in Toronto, Sound Interchange, was already booked for February.

Iommi explained to *Classic Rock*. "We had to go – the money for the studio was paid. So we had to record an album we hadn't got, because we had to write new songs with Ozzy. It was really a bad time for us. Very worrying." And the mood within the band was not helped by the bitter cold of a Canadian winter. "We were freezing to death," Butler said. "It was –18 or something. I got this cold in my ear and went totally deaf, so everything that I was playing sounded like it was underwater."

With the clock ticking, Sabbath worked at a frantic pace to finish the album on deadline. "We were rehearsing from ten o'clock in the morning to write a song and then record it in the night," Iommi

recalled. "You can't really do that. You need to live with a song a bit and try it different ways, and we didn't have that luxury. But once they were recorded, that was it."

As a result, the album was, as Iommi conceded, "a bit disjointed". There were two songs to rival the band's very best – the blistering title track and 'A Hard Road'. There was also a beautiful, jazz-influenced track named 'Air Dance', featuring future Rainbow and Deep Purple keyboard player Don Airey on piano. "That was great," Butler said. "And totally different to what we'd normally do." But this arty stuff was not to Ozzy's taste. "I remember walking in the studio and hearing this jazz shit," he said. "I thought, 'What the fuck is this?' That wasn't Black Sabbath."

Above: With his singer about to exit the band, Iommi could still raise a smile, and why not? A Black Sabbath show was always an event…

Opposite: …as demonstrated here by the athletic stage performance by Ozzy Osbourne, still able to put on a hell of a show in spite of the excesses.

"*NEVER SAY DIE!* WAS THE END OF THE BEGINNING."

Geezer Butler

Bill Ward agreed. "There were new horizons on that album," he said, "some of which were to the detriment of the band." Even more damaging was the stress of working under intense pressure. "I knew we were running into trouble," Ward said. "That was obvious." And when Sabbath returned from Toronto to undertake a UK tour in May to mark the band's tenth anniversary, their pride took a battering as they were blown off the stage by their support act Van Halen. Iommi was distraught. "The album was hard enough," he said. "But that tour with Van Halen was like the final nail in the coffin for us. It felt like the end."

Never Say Die! was released on September 28, 1978. It made Number 13 in the UK, but in the US it bombed, peaking at 69. A difficult year ended with the final dates of a US tour in December. And in early 1979, when the band started writing a new album in Los Angeles, Iommi reached the limit of his patience with Ozzy. "We wrote some riffs," Iommi said, "but Ozzy wasn't into it. He wasn't singing – he was just getting drunk all the time." Iommi came to a simple conclusion: if Ozzy couldn't sing the new songs, they would have to find someone who could.

Ozzy also threatened to leave the band again. In the end, he didn't have to. On April 29, 1979, he was fired. And as he admitted many years later: "When I got kicked out of Black Sabbath, I blamed Tony for what happened to me, and actually that was wrong. I was too fucked up. I couldn't deliver."

In October 1979, Black Sabbath announced Ronnie James Dio as their new singer. Meanwhile, Ozzy was trying to figure out what the hell he was going to do without them.

Above: A ticket from Black Sabbath's concert at the Victoria Hall, Hanley, Stoke-on-Trent, May 23, 1978. The gig followed the completion of the recording of the Never Say Die! album, which was released in September 1978.

Right: Tony and Ozzy in 1978. Ozzy's increasingly out-of-control behaviour would lead to him being fired from the band the following year.

NEVER SAY DIE!

The title came from Bill Ward. He'd been searching his imagination for a theme which would be strong and mobilizing, something to motivate and steer the band through their miserable recording sessions in Canada.

"Never Say Die!" occurred to him as his head teemed with images of Britishness – the RAF, and the national attitude. "Chin up, chaps!" – Ozzy liked that.

"Oh don't you ever, don't ever say die/Never, never, never say die again" urge the lyrics, which towards the end return to the theme of children as the potential saviours of civilization. The song itself verges on power-chord pop, and it's one of those most often cited in defence of the album by loyal Sabbath fans who have pointed to its bright pace, passable riff and up-front, untreated vocals as evidence that the old dog was not dead.

In general, the album production – credited to the band – has been widely criticized for its layered approach, its multi-tracking, reverb and other studio tricks, a debilitating mix which often submerged the vocals, and a poor sound quality.

Ozzy concurred: "I wasn't really happy with the way things were going over the last two or three albums before I left. I mean, it was really getting away from everything Sabbath had been based on in the first place. What we needed was a good, strong producer who could direct us in the studio and someone who wasn't too directly involved in the band personally. Instead, we were producing ourselves and getting lost."

He added: "We couldn't reproduce what we were doing in the studio, cos it was so overdubbed with 300 voices and all that. Tony would do seven guitar overdubs and I felt like I had to compete in a way to stay part of it... it was so bizarre... multi-tracking voices and backward harmonies... drowning people's brains with all this scientific bullshit I don't understand."

Released as a single and a taster for the album in the summer of 1978, "Never Say Die!" enjoyed a number 21 chart slot in the UK and earned Black Sabbath an appearance on "Top Of the Pops".

JUNIOR'S EYES

Ozzy rewrote the lyrics to say goodbye to his father, Jack. In its original form, this was one of the Dave Ward collaborations, and it changed little musically in the crossover. A dreary mid-tempo, it outstays its welcome as it ploughs towards the seven-minute mark in a welter of improvisation.

However, the hugely personal sentiments expressed by Ozzy endow the song with a validity it would not otherwise have deserved.

"Junior's eyes, they couldn't disguise the pain/His father was leaving and Junior's grieving again," sings a devastated son.

Left: Ozzy and Tony on the ill-fated Never Say Die! tour in 1978. Ozzy later admitted: "I was too fucked up. I couldn't deliver."

Below: What does Iommi's ferocious smile reveal? Perhaps that everything within the Sabbath camp was resting on a knife-edge at this time. The band were about to implode… spectacularly.

Ozzy has described in painful detail the heartbreak of his cancer-stricken father's last days and funeral. He told one interviewer: "They put him in a fucking closet with the fucking mops and buckets because he was on the death ward and it was too distressing for the rest of the patients. So they put him in a cot, sort of a crib thing, a giant crib.

"They strapped him like a boxer, fucking bandages on his hands, with a glucose drip going into his arm. He was stoned out of his head...

"I told my father one day, 'I take drugs. Before you go, will you take drugs? He says, 'I promise you I'll take drugs.'

"He was totally out of his mind on morphine, because the pain must have been horrendous. They had the operation on a Tuesday and he died on Thursday. No one could understand what he was talking about, because he was so out of it. He says to me – he only understands drugs as 'speed' – he says, 'Ssspeeeed.' And he died in my arms."

Ozzy continued: "When they go, they're out of their misery. What freaked me out more than anything else was the funeral. I was singing fucking "Paranoid" in the church... on Seconal [a sedative], drunk... it blew me away. All the family came that I'd never seen for fucking years, and they were making comments. In England, it's a weird scene at a fucking death. My father hated his brother Harold – my whole family's fucking nuts."

AIR DANCE

The most contentious track on the album, "Air Dance" is loved and loathed in equal measure by the Sabbath following. Those who enjoy it do so perversely, since it sounds absolutely alien, quite unlike anything the band had ever attempted. For the same reasons, it's despised by hardliners, appalled that Sabbath could even contemplate such a betrayal.

The lyrics describe a stereotypical, nostalgic scene in which an elderly lady, surrounded by fading photographs, looks back on her lost youth as a beautiful, carefree dancer. "The days grow lonely for the dancing queen/And now she dances only in her dreams," laments Ozzy.

The song's great crime was to introduce a certain jazz element, creating an atmosphere for the laid-back piano, the brass and Iommi's

lead guitar excursions. Ozzy had strong feelings about the jazz inclinations of Iommi and Ward especially: "Onstage, Tony used to go into these great long guitar solos which were like jazz. I mean, jazz at a Black Sabbath gig – ridiculous. I used to watch him from the side of the stage and cringe when Tony did that sort of thing. I used to hide. I'm not knocking him technically because I still think he's a really brilliant guitar player. But his jazz solos used to slow things down."

BREAKOUT

A brass-led instrumental, "Breakout" drove another long thorn into Ozzy's flesh. It enjoys the distinction of being described by one reviewer as "the worst Iommi has written in a long line of space-filling instrumentals".

Ozzy complained: "On the last album, on that track "Breakout", I couldn't believe it one Sunday morning when 30 guys with trumpets marched in and started playing on a Black Sabbath album. It nearly made my hair fall out."

He went further: "Tony was always trying to make the band more sophisticated. I mean, there was one time when he brought in a load of string players on a session. I walked into the studio and there were all these guys of about 50 sitting around waiting for their go. I thought to myself, 'What the hell is all this?' I mean, violinists on a Black Sabbath album! If I'd been a fan, I wouldn't have believed it."

Ozzy admitted: "I wanted to get back to good, basic, hard rock like we were known for. I wouldn't have minded doing the new stuff if it was reproduceable onstage, but it wasn't. Fucking hell, it took so long to do. It was done in three sections and joined together. No way could you do that onstage – they'd think you were R2D2. Studios drive me up the wall. After a month or two in one of those places, I feel like a bat.

"Fuck this overdubbing and all that mechanical crap, Tony Iommi playing through a jar of Vaseline or something.

"Showing up on those later albums was just each individual going a little bit more in their own direction," reasoned Bill Ward. "There were more differences going on as we were all growing... Each of us is very talented and can do a lot of things other than the phenomenon that is Black Sabbath – I see that as the four of us. We are capable of so much more as individual people. Ozzy is a great example of that."

Other tracks on *Never Say Die!* are the keyboard-heavy riff-rocker "Johnny Blade" – a portrait of the meanest guy in town – with a two-minute guitar solo beloved of some fans; the plodding, jamming "A Hard Road", which tritely talks of the harshness of life but hopes for a better future and features backing vocals from Butler and Iommi (in the only singing he ever did for Black Sabbath); "Shock Wave", whose black moon, blood red sky, blood brew, wind of mist, ghostly shadows, evil power and crawling body receive scant musical justice in this standard rock riff-and-solo work-out; "Over To You", a prog-orientated protest at the state's brainwashing of schoolchildren; and "Swinging The Chain", rock'n'rolling with a Bill Ward vocal that leaps from softly-softly familiarity into a series of primal screams as he plunders his military fixations from the viewpoint of World War II.

Above: The energetic Ozzy takes flight at London's Hammersmith Odeon on June 10, 1978, during the Never Say Die! tour.

Opposite: Brothers despite it all. The crowds had just witnessed the last gasp of the classic Sabbath line-up for the best part of the next two decades.

BILL WARD

HE HAS SURVIVED ALCOHOLISM, DRUGS AND A HEART ATTACK.
HE EVEN SURVIVED HAVING HIS BEARD SET ON FIRE BY TONY
IOMMI. LIFE HAS BEEN HARD FOR BILL WARD. BUT HE IS THE BEST
DRUMMER THAT BLACK SABBATH EVER HAD. HIS ABSENCE FROM
SABBATH'S LAST ALBUM IS THEIR LOSS AS MUCH AS HIS.

Tony Iommi made Black Sabbath the heaviest band on Earth. Bill Ward made them swing. As Iommi said in 1999: "There's been a load of great drummers in Sabbath, but nobody like Bill."

William Thomas Ward was born on May 5, 1948 in Aston, also the birthplace of Ozzy Osbourne and Geezer Butler. When the young Bill first started playing drums, his great love was jazz, in particular the big bands from the 1940s and virtuoso drummers such as Gene Krupa and Buddy Rich. In later years, he would bring something of this style to Black Sabbath.

Ward could hit as hard as any rock drummer of his age – his good friend and Zeppelin drummer John Bonham included. But he also had a broad range and a subtle touch and feel. "It's all about vibe," Ozzy once said. "Charlie Watts isn't the best technical drummer in the world, but what he does is just perfect for the Rolling Stones. And that's what Bill would bring to Sabbath. I've sung those old Sabbath songs with a zillion different musicians, but there's only one band that can really play them, and that band is the original Black Sabbath."

Ward also had additional talents, besides drumming, which were utilized on the band's early albums. He co-wrote the lyrics for songs such as 'Black Sabbath', from the first album, and 'Johnny Blade', from *Never Say Die!*. As Geezer Butler recalled: "'Johnny Blade' was about Bill's brother, who used to be in a knife gang when he was growing up." On the same album, Ward's jazz influences were prevalent on the track 'Junior's Eyes'. "We were really kicking back on that song," he said. "It's completely jazz-oriented."

There were two Sabbath songs on which he also sang lead vocal, 'Swinging The Chain' and 'It's Alright'. The latter, written by Ward alone in homage to the Beatles, was much loved by Guns N' Roses singer Axl Rose, who performed it live at the height of that band's popularity in the early 90s. As Ward said of this song: "A lot of the stuff I was writing back then always sounded a bit demonic. 'It's Alright' was the exception – and I wrote it in five minutes."

Alcohol and drugs would lead to many of the problems in Bill Ward's life. He enjoyed them greatly in the early days of the band. "There were good times," he said. "There were occasions when we went on stage loaded, when we went on stage after we'd dropped a tab of acid. We'd all be high – in front of 30,000 people! Those things did happen."

Ozzy was his chief partner in crime. "Me and Bill were the worst," Ozzy said. "Like the Drug Commandos: never come through the door where a plate-glass window will do!" Ward's continual bingeing, combined with his passive nature, brought out a cruel streak of humour in his bandmates – most famously illustrated when Iommi set fire to the drummer's beard for a laugh. Stoned out of his mind, Ward merely noted that it smelled like "good stuff".

However, by the end of that decade, Ward was burned out. He recalled: "I couldn't do it anymore – the excess. It was becoming an elephant in the room. In my mind I was young and strong and impregnable. But in hindsight, I was going by the skin of my teeth."

His state of mind was not helped when, in 1979, his best friend in the band was fired. Somebody had to break the news to Ozzy that he was out, and Ward volunteered. "The whole thing was extremely uncomfortable," he said. "I disliked my actions intensely."

Ward followed Ozzy out of Black Sabbath in 1980, and although he would briefly return for the *Born Again* album and for Live Aid in 1985, his alcoholism escalated to the point where, in the late 80s, he was reduced to begging around the Huntington Beach area of Southern California. Broke and desperate for a drink, he was, he admitted, "panhandling for nickels and dimes."

Eventually, Ward managed to get sober and put his life back together, but there was a price to be paid for all those years of drinking and drug taking. In 1998, he suffered a heart attack during rehearsals for Sabbath's reunion tour. He recovered in time to rejoin the band in 1999, and continued to tour with them until 2005. And six years later, he was once again a part of Black Sabbath as they began work on a new album.

In the end, this did not work out as Ward had hoped. He resigned from the band in 2012 in a dispute over his contract, and the Sabbath album was recorded without him. In a parting statement, he said: "I will continue to be honest and respectful to the band and our fans."

When the album, *13*, was released, Tony Iommi stated: "We get on great with Bill personally. We did try." *13* also confirmed the truth of what Iommi had said in 1999: "Nobody plays like Bill."

Opposite: A master musician, led to the very brink of death by his fatal fondness for the demon drink. Fortunately, at the time of writing the great Bill Ward has been clean and sober for over 35 years.

THE 1980S

A NEW DECADE BEGAN WITH RONNIE JAMES DIO AS THE SINGER IN
BLACK SABBATH AND OZZY OSBOURNE WORKING WITH A LITTLE-KNOWN
GUITAR PLAYER NAMED RANDY RHOADS. THE BATTLE LINES WERE
DRAWN. "WE WERE AT WAR," OZZY SAID. AND THERE WOULD BE ONLY
ONE BRIEF TRUCE – FOR THE BIGGEST MUSIC EVENT EVER STAGED…

When Ozzy Osbourne was kicked out of Black Sabbath, he was desolate. At the age of 30, he felt washed up, a loser. And he acted accordingly. For two months, he lived as a recluse, holed up in a Hollywood hotel, Le Parc, where he remained for days on end, the curtains drawn as he attempted to numb the pain of a very public humiliation via huge quantities of booze, dope and cocaine.

The only people admitted to his room were drug dealers, pizza delivery guys, the occasional groupie, and the hotel maids – until he received an unexpected visitor, Sharon Arden, daughter of Sabbath manager Don Arden. She worked for her father, and had something of the old man's bullish business sense. What she told Ozzy was straight to the point. "Talent doesn't stop because you got fired," she said. "Your fans don't desert you because you got fired either." It was exactly what he needed to hear. Sharon Arden was promptly appointed as Ozzy's manager.

Ozzy had been enraged by the news that Black Sabbath would continue without him. "I think they're really robbing the kids," he stated to journalist Sylvie Simmons of *Sounds* magazine. "If you bought a ticket to see the Rolling Stones and you get there and it's just Bill Wyman and a bunch of strangers, how would you feel? Let's face it, it's a totally different band." But in the early months of 1980, with Sharon pulling the strings, Ozzy assembled a band of his own. And with this, his career would be resurrected in spectacular fashion.

Above: Who could possibly have foreseen that Black Sabbath would come back – arguably stronger than ever before – with the mighty Ronnie James Dio at the helm?

Opposite: If you saw Tony Iommi live during the Heaven And Hell era of Black Sabbath's career, you're incredibly fortunate: the man was writing and playing like never before.

"LET'S FACE IT, IT'S A TOTALLY DIFFERENT BAND."

Ozzy Osbourne

For a brief period in 1979, Ozzy had worked with Irish guitar hero Gary Moore, formerly of Thin Lizzy. In Randy Rhoads, Ozzy found a guitarist of equal measure to Moore. Rhoads, a native Californian, was just 22 when he auditioned for Ozzy. At that time, he was a member of Quiet Riot, the LA metal band that would go on to huge success in 1983 with the US Number 1 album *Metal Health*. The first time Ozzy heard Rhoads play, he was blown away. As he recalled to *Classic Rock*: "I was thinking, either this is incredible gear that I'm on, or this fucking guy is something else!" With Rhoads at his side, the war with Black Sabbath could begin.

For three years, the battle was closely contested. With Dio, Sabbath made two brilliant albums, *Heaven And Hell* in 1980 and *Mob Rules* in 1981, both of which sold well in the UK and US. Ozzy and his band – Rhoads, former Rainbow bassist Bob Daisley and ex-Uriah Heep drummer Lee Kerslake – matched them blow for blow with 1980's *Blizzard Of Ozz* and 1981's *Diary Of A Madman*. In America, Ozzy had the upper hand.

But then in 1982, Ozzy's world was turned upside down. On March 19, during a US tour, Randy Rhoads was killed in an aeroplane crash in Leesburg, Florida. Ozzy's touring party had been travelling by bus en route to Orlando when their driver, Andrew Aycock, stopped in Leesburg, where he owned a home adjacent to an airstrip. While Ozzy and Sharon were asleep on the bus, Aycock, a licensed pilot, took Rhoads and Sharon's assistant Rachel Youngblood on a joyride in a light aircraft. Witnesses reported that Aycock twice flew low over the bus, buzzing

it, before a third attempt resulted in disaster. The left wing clipped the back of the bus, and the plane crashed into the garage of a nearby house. It was later revealed that the bodies of Rhoads, Youngblood and Aycock were identified only by dental records and jewelry.

In the immediate aftermath, Ozzy was traumatized. "In a way, you don't feel," he said. "You just shut down." But Sharon convinced him that he had to carry on. The tour was completed with two stand-in guitarists: first, Bernie Torme, previously of Gillan, then Brad Gillis of Night Ranger. And although Ozzy would struggle to come to terms with the loss of Rhoads, he kept going. Throughout the 80s, Ozzy had huge success with a string of multi-platinum albums.

For Black Sabbath, it was a different story. Ronnie James Dio left the band in November 1982, and from that point, Sabbath's career nosedived. Replacing Dio with former Deep Purple singer Ian Gillan in 1983 proved disastrous. And after the original Black Sabbath reunited for Live Aid on July 13, 1985, it was only the bloody-minded determination of Tony Iommi, the sole remaining founder member, which kept the band alive.

Even if the war with Ozzy was lost, Tony Iommi would not give up on Black Sabbath.

Opposite: Ozzy refreshes himself backstage at Live Aid.

Below: The height of the Eighties, captured in a single shot. Ozzy's sequinned costume; his bouffant hair; Iommi's shades; the successful repackaging, whether you liked it or not, of rock as a charity vehicle.

PROFILE
RONNIE JAMES DIO

REPLACING OZZY OSBOURNE IN BLACK SABBATH WAS NO EASY TASK.
RONNIE JAMES DIO JUST MADE IT LOOK THAT WAY. ON HIS FIRST
ALBUM WITH SABBATH, *HEAVEN AND HELL*, THE BAND WAS REBORN.
AND 30 YEARS LATER, FRONTING THE GROUP THAT WAS NAMED AFTER
THAT ALBUM, DIO DELIVERED HIS LAST GREAT PERFORMANCE.

When Ronnie James Dio was announced as the new vocalist in Black Sabbath in 1979, there was hostility from both the music press and hardcore Sabbath fans. Dio had a formidable reputation. He had proved during his five years with Rainbow that he was one of the best rock singers on the planet. But the man he was replacing in Black Sabbath was himself no ordinary singer.

Ozzy Osbourne was a huge star, a brilliant frontman, the people's champion; and his voice was as instrumental as Tony Iommi's riffs in defining Sabbath's sound. To further complicate the issue, Dio was an American joining a quintessentially British band.

Dio was not fazed. He knew that he could bring something new to Black Sabbath. His voice had a greater range than Ozzy's. He had his own unique style of writing lyrics: storytelling steeped in history and fantasy. Above all, he believed, with unshakable conviction, that he could make Black Sabbath great again. And he did so with the first album they made together, *Heaven And Hell*. As the review of the album in *Sounds* stated: "Ronnie James Dio has injected a whole new energy into the group. In some ways this is a new band."

Heaven And Hell would over time be recognized as one of the classic Black Sabbath albums. And in the career of Ronnie James Dio, it would rank as one of his three defining works, alongside Rainbow's *Rising* and his own band Dio's *Holy Diver*.

Ronnie had travelled a long road before he joined Black Sabbath. He was born in Portsmouth, New Hampshire on July 10, 1942, and named Ronald James Padavona. In the late 50s he played bass in his first professional group, The Vegas Kings. But it didn't take him long to take centre stage as lead singer of a new band, Ronnie & the Red Caps, later renamed Ronnie Dio & the Prophets after Ronnie had adopted a stage name appropriated from mobster Johnny Dio.

In the late 60s he formed a heavy rock group, the Electric Elves, later renamed Elf. And in 1974, after the band had recorded three albums and toured with Deep Purple, Dio got his big break. For a solo album, Purple's moody guitar hero Ritchie Blackmore hired all of the members of Elf, except guitarist Steve Edwards – and out of this was born a new band, Rainbow.

The album, titled *Ritchie Blackmore's Rainbow*, was released in 1975, shortly after the guitarist quit Deep Purple. In this moment, Ronnie James Dio came of age. In a voice that soared and thundered, Dio lit up songs such as 'Man On The Silver Mountain' and 'Sixteenth Century Greensleeves'. The following album was even better. *Rainbow Rising* is one of rock's all-time classic albums, the epitome of what is wryly termed "castle rock", with Dio imperious on the epic track

'Stargazer', conjuring up images of an ancient desert kingdom under the spell of a doomed wizard.

After a monolithic double-live album *On Stage* and a third great studio album *Long Live Rock 'N' Roll*, Dio's time with Rainbow ended in 1979 when Blackmore decided to replace him. His choice was Graham Bonnet, a singer better suited to the more mainstream hard rock that that the guitarist had in mind. But within the year, Ronnie had hooked up with Sabbath, and as he explained in 2008, this gave him more artistic freedom than he had enjoyed in Rainbow. "Tony Iommi is a genius," he said, "just like Ritchie. But Tony and Geezer gave me so much more latitude, so much more space for expression. It was just wonderful for me. Plus, on a personal level, it was great. I wasn't British, but it didn't make any difference. I came from a working class family the same as they do. So we were able to relate on those terms. And it was all about the music."

The good times did not last. Following *Heaven And Hell* and another great album, *Mob Rules*, Ronnie quit Sabbath in an argument over the mixing of the *Live Evil* album. He formed a new band named Dio, with former Rainbow colleague Jimmy Bain on bass and fellow Sabbath fugitive Vinny Appice on drums, plus 19-year-old Irish guitarist Vivian Campbell. The debut Dio album, 1983's *Holy Diver*, is a heavy metal classic. The second album, *The Last In Line*, is not far off. And in 1986, Ronnie was the lead vocalist and co-writer of the charity song 'Stars' by Hear 'n Aid, heavy metal's answer to Band Aid, an ensemble featuring the members of Dio and others from Mötley Crüe, Journey, Quiet Riot and more.

Ronnie's reunion with Sabbath for the 1992 album *Dehumanizer* was cut short when he refused to appear with the band as support act at Ozzy's "farewell" shows in 1993. But there was one final reunion in 2007, when he formed Heaven & Hell with Iommi, Butler and Appice. The band released a new album, *The Devil You Know*, in 2009. It would be the last of Ronnie's recordings released in his lifetime.

Ronnie James Dio died from stomach cancer on May 16, 2010. Geezer Butler described his loss as "heart-wrenching". Tony Iommi remembered Ronnie as "a great friend". And when Ozzy paid his respects – saying, "Ronnie James Dio was a fucking amazing singer" – he meant it.

Opposite: Poet. Lyricist. Mighty-lunged singer. Slayer of dragons. There was only one Ronnie James Dio, and we will not see his like again.

HEAVEN AND HELL

HEAVEN AND HELL
(1980)

MANY SABBATH FANS FELT THAT OZZY OSBOURNE WAS IRREPLACEABLE.
RONNIE JAMES DIO DIDN'T THINK SO. THE LITTLE MAN WITH THE BIG
VOICE HAD ALREADY PROVEN IN HIS TIME WITH RAINBOW THAT HE
WAS ONE OF THE GREATEST ROCK VOCALISTS OF HIS GENERATION.
AND WITH HIM, BLACK SABBATH WAS A BAND REBORN.

Geezer Butler would always remember the first time that Ronnie James Dio sang with Black Sabbath. In the summer of 1979, Dio was invited to the rented house in Los Angeles where the band had been living and working for many months. This was where Ozzy had spent his last days with them. And when they started jamming with Dio, they decided to try out a song that had been written while Ozzy was still around. Ozzy, his head clouded by booze and drugs, hadn't been able to find a way into this song. Dio transformed it into something magical.

Butler recalled: "I just thought, Bloody hell! We'd been sitting around in LA for six months with Ozzy doing absolutely nothing, and then Ronnie comes in and just nails it straight away."

Dio was not lacking in self-belief. He had been fired from Rainbow, but that was because Ritchie Blackmore wanted to reposition the band as a radio-friendly, hard rock act. That wasn't Dio's style. Dio knew he was good – the best of the best. And as far as he was concerned, the Sabbath job was his for the taking.

Remembering that first rehearsal with Sabbath, Dio said to *Classic Rock*: "I don't audition – I'm confident enough in myself. But it was somewhat of an audition, for all of us – I auditioned them, they auditioned me. But I knew we could be great together."

This was evident in the song that emerged from that rehearsal, a song that Dio would name 'Children Of The Sea'. It was as heavy as vintage Sabbath, yet Dio's melodic sensibility added another dimension to the Sabbath sound.

Don Arden was not convinced. In fact, Sabbath's manager wanted Ozzy back in the band. Arden ridiculed Dio, telling Iommi: "You can't have a midget singing for Black Sabbath!" But Iommi had made up his mind. Ozzy was gone. Dio was in. "I knew what Ronnie could do," Iommi said. "I'd heard the Rainbow stuff."

Butler knew it too. And yet, to Iommi's astonishment, Butler then left the band, telling them that he need time out to address problems in his marriage. In his absence, the trio of Iommi, Dio and Bill Ward continued writing. Iommi reasserted his faith in Dio by dismissing Don Arden. And in October 1979, with an album's worth of new material, the band headed to Criteria studio in Miami, where *Technical Ecstasy* had been recorded three years earlier.

On Dio's recommendation, they brought in bassist Craig Gruber, who had worked with Dio in Rainbow and Elf. It was also Dio's idea to enlist Martin Birch as producer. Birch had previously made albums with Deep Purple and had befriended Dio while producing Rainbow.

Several tracks were recorded with Gruber before Iommi persuaded Butler to return. Once in Miami, Butler added new bass parts to those tracks. But the two most important songs were recorded later, and at different locations.

The album's title track came together at the band house in LA. Iommi explained: "We converted the garage to a studio, but it was so bloody hot in there, so we had the gear set up in the house, and that's where we wrote 'Heaven And Hell' – in the lounge, jamming. It

Opposite: A giant poster promoting Black Sabbath's 1980 tour of West Germany.

"I AUDITIONED THEM, THEY AUDITIONED ME.
BUT I KNEW WE COULD BE GREAT TOGETHER."

Ronnie James Dio

MB·Touring presents

black sabbath
in concert

Special Guests: SHAKIN' STREET

2. Juni 80	Montag	Offenbach - Stadthalle		10. Juni 80	Dienstag	Würzburg - Tauber-Franken-Halle
3. Juni 80	Dienstag	München - Circus Krone		11. Juni 80	Mittwoch	Siegen - Siegerlandhalle
5. Juni 80	Donnerstag	Ludwigshafen - Eberthalle		12. Juni 80	Donnerstag	Düsseldorf - Phillipshalle
6. Juni 80	Freitag	Nürnberg - Hemmerleinhalle		14. Juni 80	Samstag	Bremen - Stadthalle
7. Juni 80	Samstag	Stuttgart - Haldenberghalle		15. Juni 80	Sonntag	Hamburg - Messehalle 8

Juni-tournee 1980

Der Vorverkauf hat begonnen.

was one of those songs that just built up as we went along." The result was a seven-minute epic with a majestic riff and the best soloing that Iommi ever played. And after that came 'Neon Knights'.

"We had all of these great songs," Dio said. "'Children Of The Sea', 'Lonely Is The Word', 'Die Young', 'Heaven And Hell'. But we needed one more to complete the album." Written and recorded at Studio Ferber in Paris, 'Neon Knights' was fast and phenomenally melodic, sung by Dio as only he could. It would be chosen as the opening song on the album – an emphatic statement of intent.

With *Heaven And Hell*, Black Sabbath was brilliantly reinvented. Dio's rich and powerful voice took their music to a different place. So too did his poetic lyrics, as Geezer Butler acknowledged. "Writing lyrics had become like torture for me," he admitted. "And Ronnie's lyrics were great – totally different to what I'd do."

Dio said of his role on *Heaven And Hell*: "I'm a different animal to Ozzy. I think in different musical terms. So it led us in a new direction. It was not Black Sabbath with Ozzy – it was something new, and it just

worked." Iommi said simply: "Ronnie gave us a new lease of life."

Released on April 25, 1980, *Heaven And Hell* was hailed as a triumph in the UK's premier rock title *Sounds*. "The Sabs are back in the saddle again with easily their finest album since *Master Of Reality*," said writer Pete Makowski. "Just sit back, turn it up and feel your brain implode as Dio, Iommi, Butler and Ward bury you in an avalanche of some of the heaviest sounds around."

And for many, Geezer Butler included, this album remains a genuine classic – one of Black Sabbath's very best. "*Heaven And Hell*," Butler said, "is as good as the first five Sabbath albums."

Opposite: The power and the glory: the Dio-fronted Black Sabbath taking no prisoners on the 1980-81 Heaven & Hell tour.

Above: Bill Ward (centre) quit the tour halfway through, unable to continue: his struggle with addiction was all-consuming. He was replaced by Vinnie Appice.

BLIZZARD OF OZZ
(1980)

**BLACK SABBATH WENT BACK TO WORK WITH RONNIE JAMES DIO
– THE FIRST IN A SUCCESSION OF VOCALISTS – WHILE OZZY SAT
IN A ROOM IN LA'S LE PARC HOTEL AND BROKE HIS HEART.**

He stayed there for more than three months with the curtains closed, surrounded by overflowing ashtrays and all the debris of a life spent indoors, only picking up the phone to send out for pizza, liquor and cocaine. "I was suicidal," he later admitted. Haunted by insecurity and a dread of ending up back at the abattoir, he degenerated into "a fucking fat, stupid mess... fat and stupid and drugged."

As legend has it, Sharon Arden magically came back into his life with some surprising news: her father Don Arden's management company had decided to drop Black Sabbath and take on Ozzy Osbourne as a solo artist. Also on offer was a deal with Arden's Jet Records.

"I was amazed," said Ozzy. "Sharon and me had nothing going at the time – in actual fact, she was seeing Tony Iommi – but there she was."

As rumours abounded throughout the rest of 1979 that Ozzy intended to call his new band Son Of Sabbath, he returned to England to put together a group called Blizzard Of Ozz. Their eponymously titled first album would rehabilitate Ozzy as a major force in heavy metal. It would also introduce a new guitar hero – the diminutive but legendary Randy Rhoads.

The first recruit was bass player and lyricist Bob Daisley, an ex-Rainbow man.

He told interviewer Jeb Wright: "People told me that I was making a mistake... that Ozzy was a burnt-out has-been and that he was a piss-head. I just had a good feeling about the whole thing. I just said, 'Fuck, I'm going to do it.' It was the sort of work that I had been looking for, you know, heavy rock.

"Ozzy did do a bit of coke and he smoked a bit of pot, but I think he drank more than anything. I used to get on his case and I think he got pissed off about it... I used to jog in those days to stay fit, and I would take Ozzy with me to get him away from the shit and to give him more of a healthy feeling."

Somewhere along the line in LA, Ozzy had bumped into Randy Rhoads – a young guitarist from Santa Monica with a band called Quiet Riot. Randy was flown to London and, from there, he travelled with Daisley to the Midlands town of Stafford, where Ozzy was living.

Ozzy said: "When he turned up, unfortunately, I was stoned out of my mind. I mean, I was on another planet. Some guy woke me up and said, 'He's here.' I looked up and Randy started playing from this tiny amp. Even in my semi-consciousness, he blew my mind. I told him to come by the next day and that he had the gig." Finding a drummer proved more difficult. Lee Kerslake, formerly of Uriah Heep – the last to be auditioned – fitted in perfectly and the jigsaw was complete, with keyboardist Don Airey recruited for the sessions.

With most of the material already written, the band retired to a residential studio in Monmouthshire, Wales, to record the self-produced *Blizzard Of Ozz* with the intention that it would be hard, heavy and straightforward.

Asked about Ozzy's attitude in the studio, Daisley told Jeb Wright that the singer was not a perfectionist: "He is to a point, but I would get very serious about the music and the production and about rehearsing and getting parts right. He used to jokingly call me Sid Serious: "Fucking come on, Sid Serious, lighten up.'"

"I am easy-going in the studio, and I like to have a laugh as much as anyone else, but I take my music serious. Randy did as well... Randy was really just starting to come alive in his playing. All due respect to Randy, he was a brilliant player, a great player and a dedicated player, but I think the chemistry between the four people brought out the best in everybody, including Randy and Ozzy."

Ozzy gives greater credit to Rhoads, describing him as "phenomenal" and remembering: "Randy was the first guy that ever gave me time. I have a lot of ideas in my head, but being as how I don't play an instrument, to put them across musically is very difficult for me. Randy had the patience and the time to hear me out and work ideas out with me..."

Ozzy also enthused: "When we were recording, he would disappear in the studio for days. I'd ask him what he was doing and he would say, 'I'm working on this solo and I still can't get it.' Finally, it would come

Opposite: Caped and wielding a crucifix, Ozzy writhes around in the studio during the photo shoot that would supply the cover artwork for *Blizzard of Ozz*.

to him and he would call me and say, 'Listen to this.' It would always tear my head off."

Randy Rhoads' innovative and emotional guitar work on the two albums he completed with Ozzy before he was killed in a plane crash is revered to this day.

Blizzard Of Ozz – with all songs credited to Osbourne, Rhoads and Daisley – was released in the UK by Jet in September 1980 and in the US six months later by Jet-CBS. It reached numbers seven and 21 respectively, and quickly achieved quadruple-platinum sales.

It was a landmark album for Ozzy and for the rock scene, which responded to the fresh and compelling vigour of this combination of bad-assed musical poke, darkly troubled lyrics, tension, dynamics, up-tempos and broad likeability. Add to this guitar virtuosity and the brain-mashing riffs of Ozzy's past, dazzling fills and runs, expressive phrasing and the odd pseudo-classical adventure and the album was a winner.

"I'm as happy as a pig in shit at the moment," beamed Ozzy. "Couldn't be happier. I don't really think about Sabbath any more... I don't care what they do."

CRAZY TRAIN

Ozzy wrote some sleeve notes for his future compilation album *The Ozzman Cometh*. He explained that "Crazy Train" – "I'm going off the rails on a crazy train!" – was about "everything I was going through at the time" and traced the song's origins to the studio in Wales.

"The studio was rumoured to be haunted by a poltergeist," he wrote. "Most days we would wake up and windows would be smashed, crockery shattered, doors were broken off their hinges and our clothes would be floating in the stream outside. The studio owner was insisting that it was us getting drunk every night and tearing up the studio, but we stuck by our story that it was always the poltergeist."

"Crazy Train" is really a peace song about how crazy it is that people are brainwashed and mind-controlled by the powers-that-be over fucking stupid religion and stuff like that," added Bob Daisley, talking to Jeb Wright. "That is why the opening lines are, 'Crazy but that's how it goes/Millions of people living as foes'. We have inherited all the bullshit from all of the cold wars and all of the crap. The young people inherited it, and back then *I* was still young."

While many fans assume that Ozzy wrote his own lyrics, Daisley retorted that he, in fact, supplied all of them for *Blizzard Of Ozz* and the following albums *Diary Of A Madman*, *Bark At The Moon*, *The Ultimate Sin* and *No Rest For The Wicked*.

Often, they were purpose-built for Ozzy to sing. Daisley said: "We started putting music together – just me and Randy and Ozzy. Ozzy had these vocal melodies and he would sing them with any words that came into his head. Ozzy and Randy sat up one night trying to write lyrics and I came down and saw what they had done... I told them, ' tell you what, I will write the lyrics.'

"What I am most proud of is "Crazy Train". Randy came up with the riff and Ozzy came up with the vocal melody and I wrote the lyrics and the musical section that Randy soloed over in the middle. It has become a rock'n'roll anthem, and I am really proud of that."

"Crazy Train" finds Ozzy's vocals and Rhoads' flashing guitar locked tight into a hard-rock groove that appealed well beyond the metal community.

GOODBYE TO ROMANCE

The slow and strongly melodic "Goodbye To Romance" stands as Ozzy's farewell to Black Sabbath and his commitment to the future. Laced with Rhoads' sympathetic and moving guitar work, it's all the more poignant for the fact that at the time he recorded it, Ozzy had no idea how promising his future really was. It's said that when he played his first concert with Blizzard Of Ozz in autumn 1980 in Scotland – the band appearing, informally, for a couple of gigs under the name of Law, prior to the tour proper – he burst into tears at the tumultuous audience reaction: it was the moment he realized he could make it on his own.

"I've been the king, I've been the clown/Still broken wings can't hold me down – I'm free again," sang Ozzy. If Daisley did indeed write the lyrics, he couldn't have tailored them better to the situation of his vocalist. The song ends on a positive note with the sun coming out to banish any lingering shadows of the past.

SUICIDE SOLUTION

With "Suicide Solution", Ozzy's past comes back to haunt him with a vengeance.

A trudging metal classic fronted by the ranting Ozzy, it was seriously misinterpreted by certain individuals who continued to associate the singer with a demonic underworld, people who only looked at the title and clearly didn't look too hard at the lyrics, which clearly warns of the perils of alcohol abuse.

This had tragic consequences: a teenager killed himself in America, and his parents thereafter sued Ozzy, alleging that their son had acted after hearing "Suicide Solution". This was not the last time Ozzy would be dragged through the courts by parents blaming him for their children's deaths.

The case was dismissed, and Ozzy said: "This kid who committed suicide – it was never my intention to write a song so a kid would put a fucking gun to his head. I copped the fucking blame." He also looked at the wider dangers: "America is getting heavy. Anything sensational, they just go for it. I'm desperately frightened that some guy's going to blow me away. Some of these guys are nuts. They want to take it too far. All it is, you know, I'm a clown. A terrible old showbiz ham... So why do they take it all so seriously?"

"Wine is fine but whiskey's quicker/Suicide is slow with liquor," stated the song unequivocally, using the word "solution" to mean "liquid" and not "answer".

Referring to the death of AC/DC singer Bon Scott, Ozzy said: "He choked on his own vomit, and I was into the same sort of thing for a while, drinking to excess. That song is a warning. I don't want it to happen to me."

Many fans have since come to accept that the song was about Bon Scott. Bob Daisley: ""Suicide Solution" is about Ozzy, because he was drinking himself into an early grave... I knew Bon Scott and so did Ozzy, and we did find out about Bon Scott's death during the recording of

that album. But I wrote the fucking words, so he (Ozzy) can say all he likes about who I wrote it about, but I wrote it about him killing himself with alcohol. It was a warning song. It's stupid to drink yourself into the ground. It is not a solution to a problem, as it is really just hiding."

No one can accuse Ozzy Osbourne of hiding from the reality of his drinking, although he frequently professed to be on the wagon – falling off again five minutes later.

"I have this little demon that keeps making me drink," he admitted in that same year. "I just love drinking and getting drunk. I'll drink anything. If it takes my fancy, I'll drink it. I'm the Dean Martin of heavy metal, I am. I'm not as mad as everyone makes out. I'm worse. I go mad on booze. I smash things up and set fire to myself. I set fire to my sleeve the other night when I fell in the fire, drunk.

"I drink Perrier water to cut my intake down. I don't want to be another rock'n'roll suicide. I laid off the booze totally for three or four weeks. I'd go into pubs surrounded by people full of beer and think, 'Was I as bad as that?' When I'm not at work, I get bored and start drinking."

MR CROWLEY

Ozzy rekindled his old, Satanic connections with a song about the infamous black magician Aleister Crowley, although it wasn't a particularly complimentary ode.

Opening with eerie organ music and with Ozzy's vocals sounding suitably haunting, the song rumbled solidly along as it accused its subject: "You fooled all the people with magic/Yeah, you waited on Satan's call..."

"I'd read several books about Aleister Crowley," explained Ozzy. 'He was a very weird guy and I always wanted to write a song about him. While we were recording the *Blizzard Of Ozz* album, there was a pack of Tarot cards he had designed lying around the studio. Well, one thing led to another and the song "Mr Crowley" was born."

Bob Daisley is happy to credit Ozzy with the idea and the title for the song. However, he has admitted to a guilty secret about the organ intro. "One of the auditions we had was a keyboard player who had an idea that went something like that. We got that idea and wrote that part for the beginning of "Mr Crowley"." But no chance of a lawsuit: "I think we changed it enough!"

Blowing any last shred of Satanic majesty that may have been clinging to Ozzy, Daisley recalled: "One night (on the first tour), there was a big line of kids who wanted to get their albums signed after one of our gigs. One kid, as he got his Black Sabbath album signed, said, 'Ozzy, are you still into black magic?' Ozzy looked at him and said, 'No, I like Milk Tray now...'"

Other tracks on *Blizzard Of Ozz* include the perennial metallic favourite "I Don't Know", Ozzy's regular reply to fans expecting him to hold the secrets of life and, especially, death; the short and tender classical guitar instrumental "Dee", created by Rhoads for his mother; the fast but filler-standard "No Bone Movies" about a porn fan; the environmentally worried "Mother Earth", which was inspired by John Lennon's "Mother" and rises from slow beginnings through a synthesizer passage to a Rhoads guitar showcase; and "Steal Away (The Night)", a heavy rocker that's distinguished only by some sterling guitar work.

Opposite: *Blizzard of Ozz*-era Ozzy performs with typical panache, and a killer frilled jerkin, at the Gaumont Theatre in Southampton.

MOB RULES
(1981)

TONY IOMMI THOUGHT THAT LIFE WOULD BE SIMPLER WITHOUT OZZY
AROUND. HE WAS WRONG. IN AUGUST 1980, MIDWAY THROUGH A HUGE
US TOUR, BILL WARD UNEXPECTEDLY QUIT BLACK SABBATH. AND TWO
YEARS LATER, FOLLOWING THE *MOB RULES* ALBUM, RONNIE JAMES DIO
WAS THINKING ABOUT A SOLO RECORD. THINGS WOULD NOT END WELL...

With the *Heaven And Hell* album, Ronnie James Dio had elevated a band that had been in decline for five years. The album hit the Top 10 in the UK and the Top 30 in the US.

Heaven And Hell had silenced the dissenting voices of fans and critics who said that Sabbath were nothing without Ozzy. And when the new Black Sabbath hit the road – beginning with a date in Aurich, Germany on April 17, 1980 – they played to packed houses. The UK tour included four nights at London's Hammersmith Odeon. The band's set-list featured five songs from *Heaven And Hell*, and Ozzy-era classics – 'War Pigs', 'Black Sabbath', 'Iron Man', 'Paranoid' – which Dio handled with authority.

In July, a US tour began with a series of huge shows. In Houston, Texas, Sabbath headlined at the 20,000-capacity Robertson Stadium, supported by Blue Oyster Cult and Alice Cooper. And there were 90,000 people at the Memorial Coliseum in Los Angeles for the Summer Blowout festival, where Sabbath appeared third on the bill beneath Journey and headliners Cheap Trick.

But for Black Sabbath, a new problem was never far away. On August 20, they were in Denver, Colorado, on the eve of another sold-out gig, when Dio had his dinner interrupted by a call from Bill Ward. "I'm leaving," Ward said. "I can't take it anymore. I don't want to be on the road." Dio cut him off: "You can't go, Bill – we have a show to do tomorrow!" Ward replied flatly: "I'm going home. I'm on my way right now." And he wasn't bluffing. He had made the call from Denver airport.

With their drummer AWOL, Sabbath were forced to cancel the Denver show and four others. They hurried to LA to find a replacement for Ward. And within five days, they had hired Vinny Appice, a New Yorker whose previous employers included star guitarist Rick Derringer and, remarkably, John Lennon.

Right: An adhesive backstage pass issued for Black Sabbath's concert at Madison Square Garden, May 17, 1982. The band were on the second North American leg of their Mob Rules world tour.

Opposite: Tony Iommi and Vinny Appice on stage at the Hammersmith Odeon, London, January 18, 1981.

"I HAD NO CLUE HOW TO GET THROUGH THE SONGS."

Vinny Appice

Appice's debut with Black Sabbath was a baptism of fire. After three days of intensive rehearsals, the band flew to Hawaii for a show at the Aloha Stadium in Honolulu on August 31. Appice recalled to *Classic Rock*: "To get me through that first show, I had a book with instructions – like, 'verse two, speed up.' And halfway through the show it started raining, and it went on the book! I'm like, *Fuck*! I had no clue how to get through the songs. The endings were a little long..."

For Geezer Butler, this gig was memorable for the wild antics of the Hawaiian audience. "That crowd was mental," he said. "There was a big fire in the stands. Somebody set a mortar off that landed backstage. And apparently there was a sniper outside the stadium, shooting at people as they were leaving!"

But they survived. Appice proved a safe pair of hands, and Sabbath continued the Heaven And Hell tour for a further six months, ending in St Austell, Cornwall on February 2, 1981.

In addition, they also managed to write and record a brand new song during a short break in December 1980. The song had been commissioned for the soundtrack to the animated film *Heavy Metal*. It was recorded at Tittenhurst Park in Surrey, the former home of John Lennon, which was then owned by Ringo Starr. Sabbath arrived at Tittenhurst just three weeks after Lennon had been murdered in New York. "That felt really strange," Iommi said. But what they created there was a song of immense power: 'The Mob Rules'. And it would inspire the title of their next album.

In the summer of '81, Sabbath returned to The Record Plant in LA with Martin Birch again as producer. The new album was built along similar lines to *Heaven And Hell*, with a juggernaut opening track in 'Turn Up The Night', and another epic piece in 'Sign Of The Southern Cross'. The quality ran deep into other great songs such as 'Voodoo' and 'Falling Off The Edge Of The World'.

Released on November 4, 1981, *Mob Rules* maintained the band's success. Another lengthy tour followed, running through to August 1982. But it was on that tour that Dio's relationship with Iommi began to unravel. Dio had been offered a deal for a solo album by Sabbath's US record company Warner Brothers. Iommi didn't like the idea. He also sensed a change in Dio's demeanour. The singer was becoming, as Iommi put it, "bossy".

Events took a farcical turn when the band began working on a live album, recorded on the Mob Rules tour and titled *Live Evil*. During the mixing process, a studio engineer informed Iommi that Dio had been altering the mix in secret, pushing his vocals to the fore. Although Dio pleaded innocence, Iommi barred him from the studio. And in the heated exchange that followed, Dio quit.

Vinny Appice went with him – to form a new band, named Dio. At the end of 1982, Tony Iommi and Geezer Butler were all that was left of Black Sabbath.

Right: Geezer, Ronnie, Vinny, Tony: three-quarters of Black Sabbath now had Italian blood. No wonder they were a hot-headed bunch.

DIARY OF A MADMAN
(1981)

THE EVENTS SURROUNDING *DIARY OF A MADMAN* WOULD CONSPIRE TO
OVERSHADOW WHAT WAS A SIGNIFICANT RELEASE FOR OZZY OSBOURNE.
THE DRINK- AND DRUG-INDUCED MADNESS THAT HE CARRIED AROUND LIKE
A TIMEBOMB FINALLY EXPLODED IN A SERIES OF OUTRAGEOUS ESCAPADES
THAT WOULD DRAMATICALLY HEIGHTEN AND DEFINE HIS NOTORIETY.

Diary Of A Madman was a companion-piece to *Blizzard Of Ozz*. Recorded hard on the heels of that debut, it consolidated Ozzy's newly won credibility as a solo performer, a leader, fearlessly beating a path into the Eighties with a vital and exciting vision of heavy metal.

Crucially, it was the second and last studio album to enjoy the work of Ozzy's guitar whizzkid, co-writer and right-hand man, Randy Rhoads, whose death would bring this period of chaos to a tragic conclusion.

Perhaps a little heavier than its predecessor and arguably more rushed, *Diary Of A Madman* is hard-hitting, often complicated, sometimes gentle and usually melodic, and Rhoads' trademark playing remains inspirational. Released in October 1981, it reached number 14 in the UK and number 16 in the US.

At the same time, Bob Daisley and Lee Kerslake were given their marching orders. Daisley maintains that this was simply a ploy to bring in ex-Black Oak Arkansas drummer Tommy Aldridge, who had been busy with Pat Travers when Ozzy first formed the band. Daisley was replaced by Quiet Riot's Rudy Sarzo.

Daisley would later return to the Ozzy fold, playing on, and writing for, a string of subsequent albums. But in spite of this, he and Kerslake would go on to sue Ozzy, Sharon and all the connected companies, returning to the courts in 2000 to demand $20 million (£13 million) in the ongoing dispute over songwriting credits and payments, and use of material.

Sharon's response was to remove their parts from *Blizzard Of Ozz* and *Diary Of A Madman* and to have them re-recorded by different musicians for the 2002 reissues – an action slammed by fans and critics alike who have accused her of tampering with history and of insulting Rhoads' memory.

Shortly after the pair's departure, Ozzy and Sharon Arden attended a marketing meeting with executives at CBS/Epic Records' offices in LA. Eager to protest at the coldness and hypocrisy of major record companies – and, more particularly, at what he saw as Epic's lack of

effort on his behalf as an associated Jet artist – a drunken Ozzy entered the conference room with two allegedly live doves, one in each pocket, and, to everyone's horror, bit the head off one bird in a flurry of feathers and spurting blood.

Ozzy has since contended that he only intended to release the doves, but on discovering that one had died, simply went for the jugular "rather than waste it".

He was asked to leave the building. "You should have seen their faces," said Ozzy, afterwards. "They all went white. They were speechless..." And as for the dove: "It tasted warm, like tomato sauce," or, "like a good hamburger."

One staffer who witnessed the event is "99.9 per cent sure the dove was alive." She said, "I was in shock... it was horrible. Personally, I thought it was an awful thing to do, even if it was a fake bird."

News of the atrocity swept America, ensuring that Ozzy's *Diary Of A Madman* tour would be picketed by animal rights campaigners – and would also be turned into a gorefest like no other through his own, and the fans', unique efforts.

The huge, foggy castle forming the stage set was the least spectacular feature of the show. More interesting was the tour dwarf (apparently the actor who played R2D2 in *Star Wars*) who was nightly pelted with pig entrails, jammed into a hole and then hanged (safely supported by a harness, it must be explained).

Never one to leave his audiences out of things, Ozzy threw 25lb (11kg) of offal into the crowd during each performance. Word travelled fast, and the fans began bringing along their own raw meat to participate in an exceptionally bloody food fight.

"It was insane, fucking hell, man, insane," exclaimed Ozzy later. "I was getting fucking chicken legs, fucking dead cats...

"One night a cop came backstage and says to me, 'Do you realize the effect you're having on these kids?' I said, 'It's just a bit of fun, what's the matter with you?' He showed me a photo of a kid waiting outside to go into the concert with a cow's head on his shoulder!"

In Ozzy's retellings of this story, the cow sometimes becomes a horse or an ox. And he has confided, and just as often denied, that he shot and stabbed with a sword the many cats he kept at home with wife, Thelma. "The nice lady from next door peered over the fence and said, 'Ah, John, I see you're back. Unwinding.'"

Master of the anecdote and the outrageous punchline, Ozzy was an image-builder par excellence. But it's incontestable that he did, indeed, bite the head off a live bat. This was when the tour rolled into Des Moines in the New Year of 1982.

"I thought it was a plastic toy," said Ozzy, recalling the hail of inanimate objects that would usually assail him onstage. "So I just grabbed this thing, bit the head off and thought, 'Fuck me! It was flapping.'"

Later remembering his unusual snack as "not very nice – all crunchy and warm", he added: "It took a lot of water to down just that fucking bat's head, let me tell you. It's still stuck in my fucking throat, after all these years. People all over the world say, 'You're the guy who kills creatures? You still do it? You do it every night?' It happened fucking once, for Christ's sake." Even more unpalatable than the bat's head

Above: Ozzy meets the late, ineffably great Ian 'Lemmy' Kilmister of Motörhead, whose songwriting skills he later employed.

Next spread: Ozzy on stage with Randy Rhoads in Rosemont, Illinois in January 1982. Within two months the guitarist was dead.

"MY FASCINATION WITH LIFE'S PHOBIAS HAVE MANIFESTED THEMSELVES ON THIS NEW RECORD."

Ozzy Osbourne

was the course of painful anti-rabies injections that the singer then had to undergo.

Slipknot's Joey Jordison was just one of the little kids growing up then in Des Moines who were simply transfixed by the episode.

Another day, another drama, and Ozzy has been typically inconsistent in his memories of his next great public offence, in February 1982. Arriving in San Antonio, Texas, he did, definitely, urinate all over the Alamo – a sacred monument to the 180-strong band of local people who died defending their state against an invading Mexican army.

Ozzy has sometimes denied the indiscretion, claiming that he was "pissed" and not "pissing", or has suggested that it was "a genuine mistake". But in his more candid moments, he has held his hands up, adding to the legend with this: "I can honestly say, all the bad things that ever happened to me were directly attributed to drugs and alcohol. I mean, I would never urinate at the Alamo at nine o'clock in the morning dressed in a woman's evening dress, sober."

There was no evening dress, and no early morning. Allan Jones, editor of *Uncut* magazine, was with Ozzy when it happened. He has confirmed: "Ozzy wasn't wearing a dress. He was wearing his wardrobe mistress' culottes and a straw Stetson. It must have been mid-to-late afternoon when we got down to the Alamo. We were pretty drunk by then, it must be said."

In his first-hand report recently reprinted by *Uncut*, Jones recalled the photo session at the famous landmark: "Ozzy's pulled down his culottes and is currently pissing quite torrentially all over the front of the shrine of Texas liberty."

Ozzy was whisked away by insulted police officers, locked up and arrested for public intoxication, for which he was fined something close to $200 (£130).

The next month, however, would bring an end to all the shenanigans. On March 19, 1982, Randy Rhoads was killed after going for a spin in a small, private aircraft piloted by the driver of the group's tour bus.

OVER THE MOUNTAIN

Lee Kerslake opens the track, and the album, with a pounding drum pattern that has since become an essential tool of the trade.

A fast-paced and vigorous introduction, "Over The Mountain" was a radio hit that showcases Rhoads' individuality as a guitarist, mixing unorthodox scales, sounds and turns of phrase into the classic traditions of hard-riffing and soloing, and making it all sound like the most natural thing in the world. As one reviewer noted, "He could actually make a song live, breathe and still sound great two decades after it was recorded."

"The first LP was good, but too much of it was a reflection of what was going through my head about Sabbath," declared Ozzy. "This is much more like what I sound like – and when I record with the new band, well, there'll be no comparison."

Sadly, the new band would not include his best friend Rhoads, and the pair's unique chemistry died with this album.

Just after its release, Ozzy revealed that *Diary Of A Madman* had been "an idea of mine for the last five years".

He continued: "I am happy with the success of my debut *Blizzard Of Ozz* album and the tens of thousands of followers that have come out to see the shows, but I think something has changed me. I keep seeing visions of my birth, my life and my death. I have become infatuated with the feeling of horror.

"My fascination with life's phobias have manifested themselves on this new record. I only hope its tracks will freeze the blood and make the flesh creep to make people understand that this is Ozzy music. If my ideas seem disordered in intellect or slightly psychotic... it is because they are. I am Ozzy Osbourne."

Lyrically, "Over the Mountain" falls slightly short of blood-freezing, although its mystical travels through "life's magic astral plane" do alight on a certain, unhappy place: "Living in a daydream – only place I had to stay/Fever of a breakout burning in me miles wide..." Still, the message is positive: unlock your own magic and fly!

FLYING HIGH AGAIN

"I can see through mountains – watch me disappear/I can even touch the sky..."

A feelgood pop-rocker, this is usually filed alongside an unapologetic Ozzy's other drug eulogies such as "Sweet Leaf" and "Snowblind".

Several years later, Ozzy compared these songs with the later, more cautionary tales in his repertoire. He said in 1985, "I suddenly realized that when I was a drug addict, I used to write things like "Flying High Again", all this shit. And the other night, I thought, 'Fucking hell, I sing one song for it and then straight after, I sing one song against it.' But the thing is, that's OK. Because that was where I was when I wrote that, so why shouldn't I do it? It's part of my life. It's part of what I am and what I will be.

"I might start singing fucking religious songs. I don't think so, but if I choose to, why not? To think you can't sing stuff from your last album because now you're a different man is bullshit. If they're good to write and good enough to hear and to buy, then they're good enough to sing onstage, you know? I'm not ashamed of anything I've done in the past."

Bob Daisley recalls the writing sessions for the album: "We just worked five days a week, all day. Randy had riffs that he was working on... it was Lee, Randy and myself. A lot of times Ozzy wasn't there, as he either had hangovers or he was off to see his family.

"I know he came up with the vocal melody for "Flying High Again". He used to have a microphone at the side of his drums and he would sing while we put the songs together."

Daisley also told Jeb Wright a story about his teenage years in Sydney, Australia, where he played in a band: "We went to the country to do a gig. This was in the Sixties, and we were all dressed in our flower-power gear. We had on fringed jackets, flowery shirts and little square glasses. We must have looked really freaky to the country people.

"I had a station wagon and as I was loading my gear after the gig, this country-looking guy came up to me and said, 'Are you going back down to the smoke tonight?' I said, 'Yeah.' To him, people in the city must have been weird and all on drugs, because he said, 'Are you going to be flying high again in Sydney town?'

"When I was writing the lyrics for "Flying High Again" I was doing a bit of coke with Ozzy and I thought, 'Here I am flying high again,' and that guy's voice came back to me and I thought, 'Fuck, that is a good title.'"

YOU CAN'T KILL ROCK'N'ROLL

Ozzy's contempt for the record industry at this time was all-consuming. It gave rise to the notorious incident in which he bit the head off a dove, and it created the acid sentiments of "You Can't Kill Rock'n'Roll".

"Ozzy had the basic idea and I wrote all the lyrics for it," said Bob Daisley. "It is just about record companies being fucking greedy and trying to tell the artist what to do. They will tell you one thing and then do something else. It was really about record companies controlling, and the industry in general."

"Rock'n'roll is my religion and my law!" cries Ozzy, flying the flag in the face of the dirty, rotten, cheating bastards he saw all around him.

"How many times can they fill me with lies and I listen, again/ Twisting the truth and they're playing around with my head – OK."

You can hear the passion in his vocals as the song, slow and filled with contrasting displays of brute force and gentleness, moves through its intricate arrangements. It's one of those that could have benefited from some judicious editing: many fans say they would have been willing to sacrifice a couple of minutes here and there across the album for the pleasure of an extra track.

SATO

The initials represent Sharon Arden, Thelma Osbourne – or so one theory goes. Certainly, the lyrics would fit. As Ozzy himself would undoubtedly agree, you should never let the truth get in the way of a good story. So we'll discount, perhaps, the other likely explanation, that the abbreviation stands for Sailing Across The Ocean.

Sharon Arden had become much more involved with the band managerially during the writing sessions for *Diary Of A Madman*, and she was particularly close to Ozzy.

He said: "She was the first person in my life who had ever given me any encouragement because in Sabbath I was the least meaningful member of the band. But Sharon came along, showed me respect and gave me encouragement – she educated me in my cleanliness and my mannerisms and my attitude and everything. She made me grow up and I just fell in love with her because she's great. And she sorted out all the business because, with business, I like to do as little as possible."

Ozzy had by now separated from Thelma, after years of forgetting where his front door was. According to one story, a drunken Ozzy

rolled home one night to find his possessions outside the house. Warned that he would be arrested if he set foot across the threshold, he walked away from the family home and from his marriage.

The scene was set for a formal relationship with Sharon. "I can't conceal it like I know I did before," sings Ozzy in a track which harks back, musically, to the earthy, rocking, bluesy heyday of Black Sabbath. "I got to tell you now/The ship is ready waiting on the shore." It is, moreover, a "ship of joy" which will "stop you failing".

Ozzy and Sharon were married on a beach in Honolulu, Hawaii, on July 4, 1982.

DIARY OF A MADMAN

With Ozzy well on his way to becoming rock's most celebrated maniac, it was understandable that fans would look to these lyrics hoping for a glimpse into the tormented mind of the genius at work.

Ozzy doesn't disappoint, pouring out a disturbing picture of confusion, frustration and manic depression – "Voice in the darkness/ Scream away my mental health," he urges, chillingly.

"I really wrote that one about myself," explained Bob Daisley, rather surprisingly. "When I was 16 I had my first nervous breakdown and it really fucked me up. I was a sensitive kid and I have always been a sensitive person. I suppose you have to be sensitive, being in the arts. I wrote the words about myself.

"Quite often we have problems and we are our own worst enemies, and that is why 'enemies fill up the pages', one by one in the diary. 'Are they me?' I am my own worst enemy."

Ozzy was reportedly bewildered at first by the musical construction. Said Daisley: "Randy had the rough idea for the song, and I came up with the title. One day Ozzy came in and we played him *Diary Of A Madman* and because it had funny timings, he couldn't get his head around it. He said, 'Who the fuck do you think I am? Frank Zappa?'

"We said, 'You sing in this part but you don't sing here. This timing goes like this,' etc. He started to like it when he got his head around it, but at first he was like, 'This is not for me.'"

It was the band's most challenging song to date, closing the album in epic style with its differing movements. Neo-classical guitar licks give way to a monstrous riff, quiet interludes erupt into violent rock explosions, and string sounds and choral chanting add to the general, unsettling air of unpredictability, underpinned by a wicked bass.

At the time, there were plans for a film of the same name. "It'll be like an underground movie, a lot like the truth," enthused Ozzy. "Not all the phoney, glamour side of rock. I hate all that posing.

"Why can't people just be people and throw up now and again? We all crap, even the Queen..."

It would've been some movie. Many years later, it turned into some soap opera...

Other tracks on the album are "Believer", whose heavy, bass-driven menace is at odds with its positive advice about self-belief; "Little Dolls", the gruesomely detailed story of a voodoo victim (believed by some to be a metaphor for alcoholism) sung by Ozzy on both lead and harmony vocals, set to an ordinary hard rock/bluesy soundtrack; and the forlorn and fairly average piano ballad "Tonight".

PROFILE
ALL OTHER SINGERS

THE HISTORY OF BLACK SABBATH BEGINS AND ENDS WITH OZZY
OSBOURNE AS SINGER. IN BETWEEN TIMES, SEVEN OTHERS HAVE SUNG
FOR THE BAND, WITH VARYING RESULTS. RONNIE JAMES DIO WAS
THE BEST OF THEM – CERTAINLY, THE BEST SUITED TO SABBATH.
IAN GILLAN THE MOST FAMOUS. DAVID DONATO WAS NEITHER…

The first singer who attempted to replace Ozzy in Black Sabbath never really stood a chance.

Dave Walker was an old friend of Tony Iommi's. The pair first met in the late 60s, when Walker was fronting a Birmingham club band named The Redcaps. In the early 70s, Walker had served in two of the UK's best-known blues-rock bands: first, Savoy Brown and then Fleetwood Mac. He appeared on Fleetwood Mac's 1973 album *Penguin*, singing lead on two songs.

He later moved to San Francisco, where he had spells with two groups that went nowhere, Raven and Mistress. He seemed an unlikely choice for Sabbath when Ozzy quit in 1977. But as Bill Ward said: "I liked Dave a lot and thought he had a great voice." Besides, Sabbath were desperate.

Walker spent a total of three months as Sabbath's singer, rehearsing a few new songs, and making one TV appearance with the band. In January 1978, Ozzy returned to Black Sabbath, and Dave Walker returned to obscurity.

Ozzy's sacking in 1979 marked the end of Sabbath's first great era and the beginning of another: The Dio Years. Ronnie James Dio saved Black Sabbath, restored the band's credibility and put his own unique stamp on their history with the classic albums *Heaven And Hell* and *Mob Rules* (see page xx, Chapter 17).

Following Dio's exit in 1982, an even bigger name was added to the Sabbath ranks – Ian Gillan, formerly of Deep Purple. The albums that Gillan had recorded with Purple in the early 70s – *Deep Purple In Rock, Machine Head, Made In Japan, Fireball* – were as legendary and as influential as Sabbath's classic works with Ozzy. Gillan had one of the most powerful and unique voices in rock. And after he left Purple in 1973, he had enjoyed further success with own band, Gillan. He was in every sense the equal of the members of Black Sabbath, past and present. But when they came together, in December 1982, the line-up simply did not work.

Gillan's stated preference was that he, Iommi, Geezer Butler and Bill Ward should form a supergroup under a new name. Sabbath's then manager, Don Arden, insisted that they continue as Black Sabbath. Arden's logic was undeniable: three of the participants were original members of Sabbath. The problem was that Gillan remained forever synonymous with Deep Purple. It was not an easy fit. And it didn't help that Gillan stuck to wearing his usual blue denim when photographed with his new bandmates in their regulation black.

Gillan recorded just one album with Sabbath, *Born Again*, released in 1983. It was followed by a performance at the Reading Festival in

which they encored with 'Smoke On The Water', to the dismay of many hardened Sabbath fans. In Black Sabbath, Ian Gillan was a square peg in a round hole. He left in 1984, and promptly rejoined Deep Purple.

His immediate successor could not have been more different. David Donato was a complete unknown, a muscular Californian who had previously worked as a mail order catalogue model, and who gigged around LA in Z-list bands Virgin and Headshaker. Donato talked a good game. Speaking to *Kerrang!* in 1984, he boasted: "I always had a picture of what the right singer in Sabbath should be – and it was me!" But it quickly transpired that Iommi was not of the same opinion. Within three months, Donato was let go.

Sabbath's next singer, installed in 1985, was another veteran of Deep Purple, Glenn Hughes. He joined the band by default, as a collaborator on an Iommi solo project that turned into a Sabbath album. Hughes was a phenomenal singer, as he had proved on Purple's brilliant 1974 album *Burn*. However, he was also, at that time, a chronic drug addict, and on his first tour with Sabbath he was fired and replaced by another unknown American vocalist whose name nevertheless had a familiar ring to it: Ray Gillen.

After that tour, Gillen stayed on to begin work on Sabbath's album *The Eternal Idol*, but quit halfway through. The album would be completed with a singer from Birmingham, Tony Martin. Again, he was an unknown. But he had a strong voice, similar in tone to Dio's. And he would go on to record another four albums with Sabbath, before the original band reunited in 1997.

In 2013, when Ozzy's first album with Black Sabbath in 35 years was finally released, Ian Gillan was in his thirty-third year as the singer for Deep Purple, as the band released its nineteenth studio album *Now What?!*

At this time, Glenn Hughes, drug-free for many years, was touring with the all-star rock supergroup Kings Of Chaos, following the break-up of his other supergroup, Black Country Communion, which had featured guitarist Joe Bonamassa and drummer Jason Bonham, the son of Led Zeppelin's John Bonham. Dave Walker was still touring with his own group, the Dave Walker Band. Tony Martin was planning a new solo album, having recorded with a wide array of acts since his last album with Sabbath in 1995. And David Donato had disappeared from public view after his post-Sabbath band White Tiger made an album in 1986.

2013 also marked the twentieth anniversary of the death of Ray Gillen. After leaving Sabbath, he had formed the hard rock group Badlands with ex-Ozzy guitarist Jake E. Lee and one-time Sabbath drummer Eric Singer. But in 1993, at the age of 32, Gillen died from an AIDS-related illness.

Opposite: Tony 'The Cat' Martin, whose work in the Nineties with Black Sabbath should not be underappreciated. He did a fine job on stage and in the studio.

Above: Ian Gillan, best known for his work with Deep Purple, who joined Black Sabbath for the *Born Again* album and tour after a drunken night in the pub.

BORN AGAIN
(1983)

IN DECEMBER 1982, TONY IOMMI AND GEEZER BUTLER FACED A FAMILIAR
DILEMMA. THEY HAD REPLACED OZZY OSBOURNE IN BLACK SABBATH. NOW
THEY HAD TO REPLACE RONNIE JAMES DIO. AND ALSO FIND A DRUMMER.
TO GET THE BAND BACK ON TRACK, IOMMI AND BUTLER TURNED TO AN
UNLIKELY SOURCE: DON ARDEN WAS REHIRED AS SABBATH'S MANAGER.

After Ronnie James Dio walked out of Black Sabbath, the first singer that Tony Iommi contacted was David Coverdale, leader of Whitesnake. In 1982, Whitesnake were hugely popular in the UK, with four consecutive Top 10 albums. But Coverdale was aiming to break the American market, and had just signed a new US deal with Geffen Records. Iommi would have to look elsewhere.

Since the news of Dio's exit had been made public in November, the band received demo tapes from numerous singers, most of them unknown. Among them was Michael Bolton, who was then struggling to get his career moving after his rock band Blackjack had fizzled out. Bolton's demo tape secured him an audition with Sabbath, at which he sang three songs: 'Heaven And Hell', 'War Pigs' and 'Neon Knights'. Iommi remembered thinking that Bolton was good, but not the right fit for Sabbath.

It was Don Arden who suggested that Iommi and Butler should talk to Ian Gillan. As the singer for Deep Purple between 1969 and 1973, the golden era of the fabled "Mark II" line-up, Gillan had attained legendary status. He was a big hitter. And as of December 1982, he was also available. His long-running band, named simply Gillan, had split up in the previous month, and secretive plans for a Deep Purple reunion had come to nothing.

Gillan met Iommi and Butler at a pub, The Bear, in the Oxfordshire town of Woodstock. A marathon piss-up ensued. It was lunchtime when they started. By closing time, Black Sabbath had a new singer. And soon afterwards they also had a drummer, when Bill Ward agreed to rejoin the band, three years after he quit to get sober. On April 6, 1983, the new line-up of Black Sabbath was announced at a media conference at La Beate Route, a club in London's Soho. The rock press promptly dubbed the band "Deep Sabbath", or "Black Purple".

The album Born Again was recorded at The Manor, a studio in Oxfordshire owned by entrepreneur Richard Branson. Two songs on the album – 'Zero The Hero' and 'Disturbing The Priest' – were reminiscent of vintage Black Sabbath, powered by the kind of grinding

riffs that Iommi had been creating since the band's inception. But, as he later acknowledged Born Again "was very different to anything we'd done before."

Simply, Gillan was too big a personality to fit into Black Sabbath. For the most part, he sounded like he was singing for a different band – namely, Deep Purple. Worst of all was his over-the-top performance on 'Disturbing The Priest', cackling like a pantomime villain. It sounded as if he was drunk.

Above: Feeling sweaty? Then mop your brow with this bespoke bit of Black Sabbath merchandise…

Opposite: Tony Iommi, Ian Gillan, Bev Bevan and Geezer Butler: the barely-appreciated Born Again line-up.

Next spread: The babyfaced Bev Bevan, previously of Electric Light Orchestra, who took over Bill Ward's drum stool for the Born Again tour.

"I DECIDED THE SABBATH EXPERIENCE COULD NOT BE A LONG ONE."

Ian Gillan

Gillan also hated the artwork for the album's cover. It was Steve 'Krusher" Joule, designer of *Kerrang!* magazine, who created the garish image of a demon baby with horns, fangs and claws. Famously, Gillan said that when he first saw the cover, he puked.

Nor were these the only problems. The moment the album was completed, Bill Ward informed Iommi that he could not commit to the band's upcoming world tour. Gillan later explained, euphemistically: "Bill's health problems got the better of him. He went back to LA to find treatment and recover." Ward's replacement was an old friend of Iommi's, Bev Bevan, the drummer for Electric Light Orchestra.

Another unpleasant surprise quickly followed. On August 7, 1983, the day that *Born Again* was released, Sabbath were rehearsing for the tour at Birmingham NEC, where they watched in disbelief as their new stage-set was being assembled. Inspired by an instrumental track on the album, titled 'Stonehenge', the set was a replica of the prehistoric monument, designed by Butler in a sketch with measurements in centimetres. However, during construction the original measurements had mistakenly been converted into inches. Sabbath had a Stonehenge that was as big as the real thing. So large, in fact, that it would not fit inside many of the venues on the tour.

Born Again was a hit in the UK. It reached Number 4 – the highest placing for a Black Sabbath album in 10 years. On August 27, the band headlined at the Reading Festival, where the stage could accommodate their Stonehenge, and where the 30,000-strong audience reacted positively to the almost surreal spectacle of Ian Gillan singing 'Paranoid', and Black Sabbath playing 'Smoke On The Water'.

From there, Sabbath headed to Europe and then America, but by the time the tour ended in March 1984, Gillan had already informed the band that he was leaving. As he later said: "I decided the Sabbath experience could not be a long one."

In April, the Deep Purple reunion finally happened. Ian Gillan was back where he belonged. Black Sabbath were once again at a crossroads. And a bizarre period in the band's history was concluded with a parody of that infamous stage set in the satirical 1984 film *This Is Spinal Tap*.

Tap had Sabbath's problem in reverse: a Stonehenge with a height of 18 inches, not 18 feet. "That was funny," Iommi said. "Our Stonehenge was funny too."

BARK AT THE MOON
(1983)

REWINDING: RANDY RHOADS AND BOB DAISLEY WERE STANDING ON A
RAILWAY PLATFORM IN STAFFORD, WAITING FOR A TRAIN TO LONDON AFTER
THE TINY GUITARIST'S SUCCESSFUL AUDITION FOR OZZY OSBOURNE.

Suddenly, Daisley had the strangest feeling. "I thought, 'One day, people are going to ask me what it was like to play with Randy Rhoads.' I had no idea that the album (*Blizzard Of Ozz*) was going to take off like it did, or that he was going to die in a few years."

Fast-forwarding: In the spring of 1982, Ozzy and his band were travelling in their tour bus from Knoxville, Tennessee, to Orlando, Florida, for a concert with Foreigner and UFO. Crossing over into the sunshine state, they stopped off near a town called Leesburg where the bus company was based; their vehicle needed some repairs.

Ozzy and Sharon slept on when the bus drew to a halt, but other members of the entourage decided to accept an invitation from driver Andrew Aycock to take a ride in his private plane, a Beechcraft Bonanza. Keyboard player Don Airey and tour manager Jake Duncan went first. Randy Rhoads and wardrobe mistress Rachael Youngblood stepped aboard for the second flight. Aycock suddenly started buzzing the tour bus, circling it three times before clipping it. The plane spun into a nearby house and exploded, killing all on board.

Drug tests later established that the pilot had taken cocaine, and there was speculation that he had started dive-bombing the tour bus because his ex-wife was standing outside it.

Kevin Dubrow from Rhoads' old band, Quiet Riot, surmised: "If they were buzzing the bus like people say, it probably meant that Randy was struggling with the pilot to stop him from crashing it."

Ozzy Osbourne stated in an affidavit: "At approximately 9am on Friday, March 19, 1982, I was awoken from my sleep by a loud explosion. I immediately thought we'd hit a vehicle on the road. I got out of bed screaming to my fiancée, Sharon: 'Get off the bus!' After getting out of the bus, I saw that a plane had crashed. I didn't know who was on the plane at the time. When we realized that our people were on the plane, I found it very difficult to get assistance from anyone to help. In fact, it took almost a half-hour before anyone arrived." It's been reported that Ozzy dragged a deaf man out of the inferno that had once been a house.

Hours later, Bob Daisley and Lee Kerslake, having heard the news, were "drunk and crying" at the bar of a club in Houston, Texas, "drinking all of the drinks that Randy used to drink, like a Grasshopper and all these sort of cocktail drinks".

Numb in the aftermath, Ozzy had to rethink his entire career. At first, he assumed it was over. He recalled: "In the few short years before Randy died, I had gone through so much. My father had died, I got kicked out of Sabbath – I was up and down, up and down. Then Randy got killed. At that point I said to Sharon, 'I can't keep doing this.'" Sharon's advice was to keep on going, because that's what Rhoads would've wanted.

"Randy was a truly wonderful guy, and I'm not just saying that because he's dead," said Ozzy in tribute. "I think, had he lived, he'd have blown the balls off Eddie Van Halen..."

He later stated: "The fondest memory of Randy Rhoads is just him. He was an incredible talent... He was a lot of fun. If ever I could say I was in love with another man, I was in love with his spirit. I mean, not in a physical sense. But he was beyond a friend to me."

And, significantly: "Randy Rhoads will always remind me of a time in my life and career when things took off again."

Facing yet another new beginning without his friend and ace collaborator, Ozzy battled through a black depression to take Sharon's advice. He recruited guitarist Bernie Tormé, temporarily, to help get the tour back on the road in April, with Night Ranger's Brad Gillis taking over for the concluding dates.

Ozzy also scrapped his existing plans for a live album featuring the Rhoads band. Instead, he released a double-set of Black Sabbath covers recorded at the Ritz Club in New York with the Brad Gillis line-up. *Talk Of The Devil*, called *Speak Of The Devil* in America, hit the stores in November 1982, charting at number 21 and number 14 in the UK and the US respectively.

Interestingly, Sabbath's own *Live Evil* album, released two months later, reported a number 13 chart placing in the UK and number 37 in the US.

Opposite: Randy Rhoads was dead. Black Sabbath had been successfully reborn without him. What else was Ozzy to do in 1983, but keep on keeping on?

Talk Of The Devil released Ozzy from his obligations to Jet Records. Now, in addition to a new label deal, he wanted to transfer his management to Sharon. Her father, Don Arden, was not too happy; he made things as difficult as possible for the couple, forcing them to buy the contract for a reputed $1.5 million (£1 million). Father and daughter did not speak again until 2001.

With Ozzy signed to CBS/Epic, It was time for another studio album and yet another cabinet reshuffle. Ex-Ratt guitarist Jake E Lee took over from Gillis. And Bob Daisley returned to the fold to succeed Don Costa. Costa had replaced former UFO man Pete Way, who'd stepped in after Rudy Sarzo returned to Quiet Riot.

Ozzy, Lee, Daisley and Tommy Aldridge together recorded *Bark At The Moon*. Released to rave reviews in December 1983, it scored substantially with chart positions of number 24 (UK) and number 19 (US).

In truth, it's a patchy album, but its emotional background is compelling; its inconsistency is both understandable and forgiveable. Ozzy himself has blamed the mixing process for the album's erratic results.

BARK AT THE MOON

"The title for this song actually came from a joke I used to tell, where the punchline was, 'Eat shit and bark at the moon,'" said Ozzy. "I'd had the vocal line for this and Jake came up with the riff. It was the first song we wrote together."

Although Ozzy receives sole writing credit for the tracks on the album, they were conceived collaboratively, with Jake E Lee also contributing "Rock'n'Roll Rebel" and Daisley claiming responsibility for most if not all of the lyrics.

For a song which arose from a joke, "Bark At The Moon" – a rousing opener – is appropriately cartoonish, a Hammer Horror werewolf story related in ghoulish detail: "Howling in shadows, living in a lunar spell/He finds his heaven spewing from the mouth of hell…"

Entering into the spirit of things for the video, Ozzy acts out a werewolf fantasy with relish, to the great enjoyment of MTV viewers. All good, clean, trick-or-treat-style fun – or so one might imagine.

In Canada, however, a 20-year-old man "felt strange inside" when he heard it. He felt so "strange" that, finally, he stabbed to death a 44-year-old woman and her two sons.

James Jollimore, from Halifax, committed the murders on New Year's Eve 1983. One of his friends revealed in court: "Jimmy said that every time he listened to the song ("Bark At The Moon"), he felt strange inside. He said when he heard it on New Year's Eve, he went out and stabbed someone."

This is a cross that Ozzy has had to bear throughout his career. While distraught parents have accused him of encouraging their children to kill themselves or others, Ozzy has rather acted as a magnet for the sort of teenagers who were already likely to commit such acts.

As he said himself: "Parents have called me and said, 'When my son died of a drug overdose, your record was on the turntable.' I can't help that. These people are freaking out anyway, and they need a vehicle for the freak-outs."

"Suicide Solution" had triggered a spate of deaths. By the turn of the Nineties, Ozzy had been sued by three separate families, each alleging that the song was to blame for the suicide of their child.

The first was a 19-year-old Californian youth called John who shot himself in the head while listening to "Suicide Solution". When his body was found, he was reportedly still wearing his headphones. Eric, a 14-year old Minnesota fan of Ozzy and Sabbath, turned a gun on himself the day after allegedly holding a séance in which he tried to contact dead rock stars.

Ozzy was further accused of sneaking subliminal messages on to his albums and of introducing 'hemisync' tones, which are created by soundwaves and are said to influence the listener's responses.

An attorney called Thomas Anderson, representing the family of John, contended that "Suicide Solution" contained a subliminal message recorded at one and a half times the usual speed of speech – "Why try, why try? Get the gun and try it! Shoot, shoot, shoot!" – and hemisync tones which made John susceptible to the "instruction".

Ozzy's defence retorted that this was bollocks and that, furthermore, Ozzy was entitled to write about whatever he wanted. The case went all the way to the appeals court, which upheld the decision in Ozzy's favour. The following lawsuits against Ozzy were also dismissed.

"I swear on my life I never said, 'Get the fucking gun,'" insisted Ozzy. He also explained: "I can't take responsibility for it. Causing their deaths was not my intention. If they think so, then I feel sorry for them too. You've got to try and ignore it, because around each corner there lurks another writ…

"What makes it even more annoying is that it's often done with the ulterior motive, such as a husband who's running for President, and they want to get as much publicity for their campaign…

"What's the difference between records and horror films? It's all entertainment, yet film directors aren't held responsible for deaths like we are. It's just so annoying."

More recently, he declared: "I can't even fart without someone saying it caused their cat to jump on a fire. I did this controversial chat show in America and they were saying my music causes kids to fucking go satanic and all this crap. In America, one of the craziest nights of the year is Halloween when they all dress up as fucking gooks and freaks and monsters and whatever. Yet, when I do it every night of the week onstage, they term me a fucking anti-Christ. Take that Madonna video with those burning crosses ("Like A Prayer") – I'd have my arse nailed to a fucking cross if I did that."

NOW YOU SEE IT (NOW YOU DON'T)

Another people-pleasing hard-rocker, "Now You See It (Now You Don't)" simply heaves with sexual allusions – "Can I ask a question, d'ya think that you can take a blow?/That is why I always come and go, yeah."

This is unusual for Ozzy, who was never the greatest champion of groupies and their services. He once memorably remarked: "People say, 'Brilliant! Chicks! All the dope! All the booze! You have parties every night!' But it gets boring. I got to the point where I said, 'Why am I doing this?' I'm screwing some groupie and I think, 'What fucking disease have I caught now?' You know, shitting myself, every two seconds looking at my dick seeing if it's still on me… it's absolutely not worth it for me. Half the time I wouldn't know whether I'd done it or not because I was so fucking out of it, and I'd get so guilty I'd get fucked up again."

More recently, he declared: "In the old days when I used to drink, I'd wake up in the morning thinking, 'I don't know my name, I don't know where *you're* from and I know I'm not the first guy you've done this week.' Then when AIDS started, I just thought, 'Forget it.' I was seeing guys coming out of the clap clinic thanking God that they'd only caught syphilis."

CENTRE OF ETERNITY

Caught in some sort of black hole, Ozzy describes the place right in the middle of infinity where, "There's no present, there's no future, I don't even know about the past..." He marries this to a riotous up-tempo that finds Jake E Lee kicking hard into his new role in the band.

It was an unenviable task, stepping into the vacancy left by the adored Randy Rhoads, and when Lee received his first call about the job, he didn't want to know. Cautiously changing his mind, he tried out along with 24 other hopefuls, ended up on a shortlist of three and almost blew his chances by arriving 45 minutes late for the final audition.

He told writer Steven Rosen: "Some guy said Ozzy almost walked out the door. He said, 'Fuck it. If this guy doesn't care enough to show up on time and he's going to be this kind of problem, forget it. I don't care how good he is.'"

Lee had no idea how he'd be received as Randy's replacement. He said, "If somebody comes up to me and goes, 'Man, you're number one, you're the best guitar player in the world,' I start feeling stupid. I go, 'Nah, there are guys better than me.' But if somebody comes up and says, 'You really suck, you're nothing compared to Randy,' then I go, 'Hey, fuck you. I'm good. I'm probably ten times better than you'll ever be.'"

Bob Daisley said: "Nobody knew how Ozzy's career was going to go at that time, because Randy was dead. It was going to be a whole different ballgame. I think Jake E Lee did a good job of filling Randy's shoes. I thought he was a great player. Ozzy has had other players who were a bit of a copy of Randy, either image-wise or playing-wise, or 'I used to be a pupil of Randy' or whatever. Jake E had his own style and his own sound. He didn't play like Randy, although he did play the Randy stuff very well. He did an admirable job. And I think the album turned out very good."

SO TIRED

A big, orchestral ballad with piano and a lot of melody, this portrayal of lost love was treated to a video which Ozzy, for one, will remember for a long time.

In one scene, a mirror shatters as Ozzy stands in front of it, clenching his fists. But during filming, someone over-estimated the strength of the charge which was set off to shatter the mirror: the glass exploded into Ozzy's face.

The song, meanwhile, has divided critics and fans alike. One reviewer proposed that it was "maybe the best ballad of Ozzy's career", while another pronounced it "dismal".

Among its detractors is none other than Jake E Lee who confessed to Steven Rosen: "The strings on "Bark At The Moon" I hated. "So Tired" I hated."

Lee was not entirely comfortable with his place in the scheme of things. He said: "On *Bark At The Moon*, I approached it really cautiously, because I was the new guy and I could be out any second, so I just

played him (Ozzy) riffs and if he liked the riff, then the whole band would work on it.

"I didn't argue too much if I didn't like the way something was coming out. I'd go, 'I don't really like this.' And they'd go, 'Well, what do *you* know?' And I'd go, 'I don't know anything...'

"I'd present something and they'd fight, debate, say it sucked or whatever. Everybody contributed a little bit, and it didn't necessarily come out the way I imagined it would."

In another interview, Lee complained that the band did not allow him time to experiment with different guitar sounds: "Once we all arrived at something, they said, 'Do all the songs with this tone.' Well, I like variety and I like to have the creative freedom to search for the right guitar, the right amp, the right sound for any particular solo or song."

Other songs on the album are the synth-based "You're No Different", a retort to critics; the raucous "Rock'n'Roll Rebel", reasserting Ozzy's outlaw stance; the self-explanatory "Slow Down" (on the US version only), an average rocker; "Waiting For Darkness" which is uneventful, despite its stabs at creative melody; and the UK track, "Spiders", especially for arachnophobics: "Creepy crawly things filling up your bed/Soon you'll feel him crawling through your brains..." In the end, of course, "The spider's really me..." and "There's no escape the spiders in your head."

Above: "Fur" heaven's sake (and hell's too): Geezer and Tony dress up warm at what appears to be Castle Dracula.

Next spread: The Bark At The Moon European tour line-up, 1983: Don Airey (keyboards), Bob Daisley (bass), Ozzy, Carmine Appice (drums), Jake E. Lee (guitar).

PROFILE
ALL OTHER BAND MEMBERS

IN ALL THE YEARS THAT TONY IOMMI HAS LED BLACK SABBATH, HE HAS
OVERSEEN NUMEROUS PERSONNEL CHANGES – FOR BETTER AND FOR WORSE.
BEYOND THE ORIGINAL AND CLASSIC LINE-UP, SEVEN LEAD SINGERS AND
14 OTHER MUSICIANS HAVE COME AND GONE. SOME OF THEM RECORDED
ALBUMS WITH SABBATH. OTHERS ONLY TOURED WITH THE BAND.

The original line-up of Black Sabbath was first broken when Dave Walker briefly replaced Ozzy in the winter of 1977/78. The next time this happened, in 1979, it was Ronnie James Dio who took over as singer. Rather less dramatic was the arrival of Geoff Nicholls, also in 1979.

Nicholls had something in common with the founding members of Black Sabbath. He was born and raised in Birmingham. Moreover, he was a good friend of Iommi's. In 1977, Iommi had produced the debut album by the band Quartz, in which Nicholls played guitar. Subsequently, Quartz had supported Sabbath on a UK tour.

When Sabbath first started working with Dio in '79, Iommi brought Nicholls in to play bass during Geezer Butler's temporary absence. Nicholls stayed on to become the band's keyboard player, appearing on the *Heaven And Hell* album and providing the atmospheric intro to one of the standout tracks, 'Die Young'. He continued to record and tour with Sabbath until 1995, although for much of that time he was not credited as an official member of the band, and during shows he would play offstage. He died of lung cancer in 2017.

It was on the Heaven And Hell tour in 1980 that drummer Vinny Appice joined Sabbath as a last-minute replacement for Bill Ward. Vinny was the younger brother of Carmine Appice, a drummer famed for his work with Vanilla Fudge, Cactus, Jeff Beck and Rod Stewart. Vinny's powerful style was illustrated by his debut recording with Sabbath on the *Mob Rules* album in 1981. He also featured on the controversial *Live Evil* album before quitting Sabbath with Ronnie James Dio to become a founder member of the band Dio. Vinny appeared on the classic Dio albums of the 1980s: *Holy Diver, The Last In Line* and *Sacred Heart*. He returned to Sabbath, with Ronnie, for 1992's *Dehumanizer*. From 2006 to 2010, he was a member of Heaven & Hell alongside Dio, Iommi and Butler. And in 2013 he reunited with the two other surviving members of Dio, guitarist Vivian Campbell and bassist Jimmy Bain, to perform the band's classic material under the name Last In Line.

Sabbath's next new drummer after Appice was Bev Bevan, and he also came in as a replacement for Bill Ward, who had recorded the *Born Again* album in 1983 only to pull out of the following tour. Bevan, another Brummie, had an impressive CV as a founding member of The Move and Electric Light Orchestra. He had played on all of the great ELO albums of the 70s, including the multi-million selling *Out Of the Blue*. After completing the Born Again tour, Bevan left Sabbath to rejoin ELO.

In 1985, when Iommi began work on a solo album, Iommi enlisted Eric Singer, a drummer from Cleveland, Ohio, and Dave "The Beast" Spitz, a bassist from New York. When that album, *Seventh Star*, was

rebranded as a new Black Sabbath release, Singer and Spitz became full members of the band.

During the recording of the next album, *The Eternal Idol*, Spitz was replaced by Bob Daisley, a former member of Rainbow and Ozzy's solo band. Spitz made a brief return to Sabbath on the following tour, but was replaced after seven shows by Jo Burt, who had worked with Freddie Mercury on the Queen singer's solo album *Mr. Bad Guy*. Eric Singer left Sabbath after *The Eternal Idol* to tour with Gary Moore. In 1988 he reunited with ex-Sabs vocalist Ray Gillen in Badlands, and in 1991 he became the drummer in Kiss. Singer was sidelined when the original line-up of Kiss reformed in 1996, but he rejoined the band in 2001. In the 2000s he also recorded three albums with Alice Cooper.

The drummer for Sabbath's 1987 tour in support of *The Eternal Idol* was an unlikely choice. Terry Chimes was an original member of iconic punk rock group the Clash, and played on their seminal 1977 debut

album. He also starred in Johnny Thunders and the Heartbreakers, Generation X and Hanoi Rocks. Chimes left Sabbath after the 1987 tour and later developed a new career as a chiropractor.

In 1988, one of rock's most legendary drummers joined Black Sabbath. Cozy Powell (real name: Colin Flooks) had made his name in the early 70s as a member of the Jeff Beck Group. In 1974, as a solo artist, he had a top three hit in the UK with 'Dancing With The Devil'. And in 1975 he joined Rainbow, with whom he recorded the classic albums as *Rising, Long Live Rock 'N' Roll* and *Down To Earth*. In the early 80s he played with the Michael Schenker Group and Whitesnake, and then substituted for virtuoso Carl Palmer in a version of ELP – Emerson, Lake & Powell. Cozy played on three Sabbath albums, *Headless Cross, Tyr* and *Forbidden*. He died in a car crash on April 5, 1998, at the age of 50.

Another former member of Whitesnake, bassist Neil Murray, was recruited for Sabbath's Headless Cross tour in 1989. Murray was with Whitesnake from 1978 to 1982 – the band's golden era, marked by great albums such as *Lovehunter, Ready An' Willing* and *Live... in the Heart Of the City*. Murray had left before Cozy joined Whitesnake, but in Sabbath they forged a strong partnership, even if their last album with Sabbath, 1995's *Forbidden*, was a write-off.

The last man in before Black Sabbath reunited with Ozzy in 1997 was Bobby Rondinelli – like Cozy Powell, a former drummer in Rainbow. Rondinelli recorded one album with Sabbath, 1994's *Cross Purposes*, although he returned for the Forbidden tour in 1995.

Mike Bordin was Sabbath's drummer for the Ozzfest tour in the summer of '97 – the first reunion shows with Ozzy. Formerly a member of Faith No More, Bordin was at that time in Ozzy's solo band. In late 1997, Bordin made way for Bill Ward and the completion of Sabbath's original line-up. He rejoined the reformed Faith No More in 2009.

In 2013, following the release of the *13* album, Black Sabbath began a world tour with Tommy Clufetos on drums and Adam Wakeman on keyboards. Clufetos had joined Ozzy's solo band in 2010, after previous stints with Ted Nugent, Alice Cooper and Ron Zombie. In Bill Ward's absence, Clufetos first performed with Sabbath in 2012, but for the recording of *13* he was overlooked in favour of Rage Against The Machine's Brad Wilk.

Adam Wakeman had also been a member of Ozzy's band, alongside Clufetos, for the 2010 album *Scream*. And his involvement with Sabbath carried an echo of the band's distant past. Back in 1973, Adam's father, the legendary Rick Wakeman, had played piano and synthesizer on 'Sabbra Cadabra', one of the most famous songs from *Sabbath Bloody Sabbath*.

Opposite: The great drummer Cozy Powell, who appeared on four Black Sabbath albums; he died in a car accident in 1998.

Above: Drummer Vinny Appice replaced Bill Ward who quit the band in 1980, saying: "I can't take it anymore. I don't want to be on the road."

SEVENTH STAR

(1986)

AFTER IAN GILLAN LEFT BLACK SABBATH, TONY IOMMI AND GEEZER BUTLER TRIED IN VAIN TO GET OZZY BACK THE BAND. BILL WARD CAME – AND WENT AGAIN. GEEZER QUIT. AND IOMMI DECIDED TO PUT SABBATH ON ICE AND MAKE A SOLO ALBUM. ONLY THINGS DIDN'T QUITE TURN OUT AS PLANNED…

There was no way that Ozzy was going to rejoin Black Sabbath in 1984, even if he had wanted to – and he didn't. The plain truth was that Ozzy didn't need Sabbath. Although the death of Randy Rhoads in 1982 had a devastating effect on him, Ozzy had bounced back with a new guitar player, Jake E. Lee, and another massive hit album in *Bark At The Moon*.

Moreover, a deal between Ozzy's manager and the band's manager was never going to happen. At this stage, Sharon Osbourne, who had married Ozzy in July 1982, was estranged from her father Don Arden. She wouldn't speak to him, let alone go into business with him.

After their approach to Ozzy was rebuffed, Iommi and Butler auditioned several other singers. These included Ron Keel, who would go on to have a moderately successful career with his own band Keel, and another American, David Donato, who rehearsed with Iommi and Butler for a few weeks and recorded a couple of new songs with them. Donato was even announced as the new singer in Black Sabbath, with an interview and photo shoot published for *Kerrang!* But this was Don Arden's doing, not Iommi's, and a second announcement soon followed: Donato was out.

Iommi was delighted when Bill Ward returned to the band in the spring of '84 – and deflated, but not surprised, when Ward bailed again in the summer. A bigger shock came when Geezer left soon after Bill. Geezer had been out of the band before, but this time it left Iommi completely isolated. Black Sabbath was now a one-man band.

Having led Sabbath for 16 years, through good times and bad, Iommi couldn't bear to think about putting together yet another new version of the band. Instead, he chose to make a solo album, and started writing songs with Geoff Nicholls, the keyboard player who had joined Sabbath as an unofficial fifth member in 1980. At first, Iommi planned to record these songs with a variety of high-profile singers he was friendly with: Robert Plant, David Coverdale and Rob Halford of Judas Priest. Contractual issues made this impossible, however. Iommi then worked for a short time with an unknown singer, Jeff Fenholt. That didn't work out either.

By the spring of 1985, Iommi was still trying to figure out how to complete the album when the organizers of Live Aid asked if Black Sabbath would reunite with Ozzy for the event on July 13. All four original members agreed. In typically irreverent fashion, Ozzy joked to the media that Sabbath would celebrate Live Aid's cause – raising money for famine relief in Africa – in a novel way. They would, he said, perform a song from the musical *Oliver!*: 'Food Glorious Food'.

On the day, they wisely stuck to their own material. Appearing at the US show at JFK Stadium in Philadelphia, which ran in tandem with the UK show at London's Wembley Stadium, Sabbath played three classic songs: 'Children Of The Grave', 'Iron Man' and 'Paranoid'. It was not their greatest performance. On the previous night, Iommi got so drunk with Ozzy that he had, in his words, "a dreadful hangover". And there was no talk of a permanent reunion.

Shortly after Live Aid, Iommi was shocked to discover that Geezer had joined Ozzy's band. That was a kick in the balls. But at least he had an album to focus on, for which he found what he thought was the perfect collaborator. For his solo album, he enlisted Glenn Hughes, who had starred as bassist and second lead vocalist in Deep Purple in the mid-70s.

"Glenn is an amazing singer," Iommi said. "Very soulful." Hughes' voice was well matched to the material Iommi was writing for his solo album – less heavy metal, more hard rock. The singer did, however, come with baggage. Iommi was himself using cocaine on a regular basis, but as he told *Classic Rock* many years later: "Glenn had dealers coming from all over. We'd shoo them off. But the drugs always seemed to get to him. He was difficult!"

The album, titled *Seventh Star*, was finished in August 1985 with Hughes singing on all of the tracks bar two instrumentals. The other featured musicians were Geoff Nicholls, drummer Eric Singer and bassist Dave "The Beast" Spitz. Iommi was happy – until, that is, Don Arden informed him that his record company contract demanded a new Black Sabbath album, and that *Seventh Star* would have to be it.

A partial compromise was reached. The album, released on January

28, 1986, was credited to Black Sabbath Featuring Tony Iommi. Nevertheless, Iommi was furious. He had created something different on *Seventh Star*, with classy songs such as 'No Stranger To Love' and the blues-based 'Heart Like A Wheel'. And yet, with Black Sabbath's name on the album, it was reviewed as such, with *Sounds* writer Steffan Chirazi concluding that Iommi had completely lost the plot, making reference to "the LA smog in Tone's head".

Seventh Star was a flop, and there was another disaster ahead. When Iommi took the Seventh Star band out on tour as Black Sabbath, he had to find another new singer after only five gigs ...

Above, main: The last man standing: by the time of *Seventh Star*, Tony Iommi was the sole remaining founder member of Black Sabbath.

Above, inset: Issued to "Local Crew", this adhesive backstage pass granted access to the stage and backstage. Due to band politics, note that the band is described as "Black Sabbath featuring Tony Iommi".

Next spread: Black Sabbath's Seventh Star was their 12th studio album. Released in January 1986, the album was not well received and was considered a flop.

THE ETERNAL IDOL /
HEADLESS CROSS
(1987 / 1989)

OVER THE YEARS, TONY IOMMI HAD A LOT OF TROUBLE WITH
SINGERS – IN THE LATE 80S, ESPECIALLY SO. ONE WAS FIRED
FOR BEING OUT OF HIS MIND ON DRUGS. ANOTHER WALKED OUT
HALFWAY THROUGH AN ALBUM. BUT THEN, IOMMI FOUND SOMEONE
WHO WAS COMMITTED TO BLACK SABBATH 100 PER CENT.

Glenn Hughes prepared for Black Sabbath's 1986 US tour in a somewhat unorthodox manner.

In the first week of March, during band rehearsals in Los Angeles, Hughes narrowly avoided arrest following an incident at the Sunset Marquis hotel. Having snorted 15g (½ ounce) of cocaine in his room, he had run amok in the hotel lobby, jumping on to the reception desk and tearing off his t-shirt with a knife.

The next evening was equally eventful. Relocated to a different hotel in Hollywood, Hughes embarked on another coke binge with Sabbath's tour manager John Downing. It ended with the two men fighting each other, Hughes being knocked out and sustaining a broken nose.

On March 14, the band played a small showcase gig in Hollywood. Hughes struggled though it. But a week later, when the tour opened in Cleveland, Ohio, it was clear to Iommi that his singer was a liability.

Dave Spitz, Sabbath's new bass player, told Iommi about a singer from New York with a name that was uncannily similar to a former Sabbath vocalist: Ray Gillen. Without Hughes' knowledge, Gillen rehearsed with the rest of the band on March 24, before a show in New Jersey. Just two days later, Glenn Hughes performed for the final time with Black Sabbath in Worcester, Massachusetts. Iommi felt bad about firing his friend, but Hughes had only himself to blame. As he later conceded: "I wasn't able to do my job properly."

Like Vinny Appice before him, Ray Gillen was thrown in at the deep end, making his debut as Black Sabbath singer on March 29 in New Haven, Connecticut. He saw out the remainder of the tour, through to June. And Iommi was sufficiently impressed to retain Gillen for a new Sabbath album.

The Eternal Idol would be the thirteenth studio album of the band's career, and Tony Iommi would be cursed by bad luck throughout its creation. When Don Arden was subject to an investigation over tax,

Iommi felt obliged to help. He donated a large sum – by his estimation, £60,000 – which he never recovered. And then, requiring a replacement for Arden, Iommi made a decision that he later described as "stupid". He rehired Patrick Meehan, the manager that Sabbath had dismissed amid so much acrimony in 1975. Perhaps inevitably, Meehan would be gone before *The Eternal Idol* was released. So too would Ray Gillen, much to Iommi's embarrassment.

In October 1986, during the initial stages of recording at Air Studios on the Caribbean island of Montserrat, the band's producer Jeff Glixman pulled Iommi aside and told him that Gillen wasn't cutting it. Glixman said that Iommi needed a new singer. Iommi disagreed. Instead, he got a new producer, replacing Glixman with Chris Tsangarides, who had worked as an engineer on earlier Sabbath albums, and had produced Thin Lizzy, Anvil and Tygers Of Pan Tang.

Soon after, Dave Spitz left the band due to personal reasons. Iommi promptly brought in Bob Daisley, formerly of Rainbow and Ozzy's band. But the faith that Iommi had placed in Gillen would not be reciprocated. In early 1987, when the band headed to London to complete the album at Battery Studios, Gillen left Sabbath for what he considered a better prospect – joining ex-Whitesnake guitarist John Sykes in Blue Murder.

Once more, Iommi turned to a singer with no real track record. Tony Martin, nicknamed "The Cat", had passed through a few small-time rock bands in his native Birmingham, among them Orion and The Alliance. Being a Brummie counted in his favour. He also had a voice that was not dissimilar to that of Ronnie James Dio. Martin auditioned at Battery Studios, singing a couple of the new songs. Iommi liked what heard, and had Martin record new vocal parts for the album.

The Eternal Idol was finally released on November 1, 1987. Certainly, it was not the success that Iommi had hoped for. On the US chart, it

> ## "GLENN HAD DEALERS COMING FROM ALL OVER. WE'D SHOO THEM OFF. BUT THE DRUGS ALWAYS SEEMED TO GET TO HIM. HE WAS DIFFICULT!"
>
> *Tony Iommi*

peaked at Number 168. Subsequently, Black Sabbath would be dropped by Warner Brothers in the US, and by Vertigo in the UK. Even so, the album was not a complete failure. Its best tracks – 'The Shining', 'Ancient Warrior' – had a power, a feel, which was quintessentially Black Sabbath. And if Tony Martin was finding his way on this album, there was better to come on the follow-up.

Headless Cross was released via the band's new label, I.R.S., on April 24, 1989. There was also a new drummer in Sabbath: Cozy Powell, a legendary figure, formerly of Rainbow, the Michael Schenker Group and Whitesnake. Playing bass on the album was session musician Larry Cottle. On one of the standout tracks, 'When Death Calls', there was a guitar solo by Queen's Brian May. And at the centre of it all was the burgeoning partnership between Iommi and Martin.

As a fully fledged member of the band – now, significantly, a co-songwriter – Martin excelled on an album that would be acclaimed as the best that Sabbath had ever made without Ozzy or Dio. In the classic Sabbath tradition were songs such as 'Nightwing' and the atmospheric title track. *Headless Cross* sold better than *The Eternal Idol*. More importantly, it went some way towards restoring Black Sabbath's credibility.

Left: Tony Iommi at the Palladium, New York, on the 1989 Headless Cross Tour. The album would be acclaimed as the best that Sabbath had ever made without Ozzy or Dio.

NO REST FOR THE WICKED
(1988)

OZZY WAS FACING A MUTINY. HE, BOB DAISLEY AND JAKE E LEE HAD STARTED WORK ON MATERIAL FOR *THE ULTIMATE SIN*, FOLLOWING THE DEPARTURE OF DRUMMER TOMMY ALDRIDGE.

Sharing an apartment with Ozzy, Lee found the singer's unpredictability difficult. Lee's method of working was to stay at home and write songs whereas Ozzy would disappear for whole weekends, or come staggering back in the early hours of the morning and expect the guitarist to get up and start writing on demand. This added to Lee's existing musical frustrations.

During this period, Ozzy spent some time in rehab in one of his frequent attempts to straighten himself out, and was obviously in a fragile condition.

Bob Daisley recalls a furious row: "We were writing a lot in Palm Springs. Jake and I put the music together. Ozzy was in the Betty Ford centre for his alcohol and drug problem. We did some rehearsals and then we were in London to audition drummers...

"We'd been rehearsing and putting the songs together during the week and Ozzy didn't come into some of the rehearsals. When we got into the demos – cos the record company wanted to hear some of the stuff we were doing – he wanted to start changing things, he'd started smoking pot and he was drinking.

"I said, 'Ozzy, look – fucking hell, we've got limited time here. We've got to come up with something to play the record company. Now you want to change stuff... you should've come to rehearsals and we could have done it then.'

"He got all pissed off, and we ended up in an argument. By the end of the night, it was like, 'Fuck you! And you can take fucking Jake with you.' Jake stayed, but I left.

"Then I got a phone call about six weeks after that, saying, 'We've finished the music part of the writing. Will you write the lyrics for the album?'" So I wrote the lyrics for *The Ultimate Sin* at home with tapes that they sent me."

Ozzy recorded the album with Lee, keyboard player Mike Moran and a new rhythm section – bassist Phil Soussan, replacing Daisley, and new drummer Randy Castillo, formerly of Lita Ford's band. Released in February 1986, it was a Top 10 smash in both Britain and America – yet critics, fans and even Ozzy himself agree that it was really a bit of a dog.

Lyrically, it sweeps a familiar landscape, seeking out the common ground between Ozzy and his fan following: hedonism ('Lightning Strikes'), criticism ('Never Know Why'), ruthless ambition (the title track), inner turmoil ('Secret Loser'), psychopathic insanity ('Shot In The Dark') and the threat of nuclear war: "Killer Of Giants" warns that man will destroy the world as a logical result of the arms race, while "Thank God For The Bomb' argues for the nuclear deterrent.

Musically, *The Ultimate Sin* reflects the instability around the band that recorded it. Ozzy plays to the gallery with a slightly subdued bravado, the rock is heavy and the guitar is distorted, grinding and loud but focused and obedient as Lee chops out his chords, riffs and solos. All the songs sound very similar, a layer of Eighties hairspray the only thing holding it together and masking the underlying whiff of ambivalence.

Ozzy blamed producer Ron Nevison, stating: "Although there were good songs on that album, working with a producer like Ron Nevison wasn't a very enjoyable task for me. He changed the whole colour of the album from the way I thought it was going to sound. It was like being in the Boy Scouts... when I think of it, I remember a very sterile environment. I don't have fond memories of that project."

Unhelpfully, censorship raised its head yet again: the original sleeve artwork was pulled because it featured three crucifixes and a knickerless woman. (Prior to this, 'Talk Of the Devil' had been stickered in shops because the raspberries coming out of cover-boy Ozzy's mouth looked like clotted blood. He recalled every copy, rather than have the sleeve censored.)

Looking to the future, Ozzy decided that he liked his drummer but could live without the others: Lee and Soussan both left with harsh words ringing in their ears.

"Phil Soussan was a fucking terrible bass player," blasted Ozzy. "And Jake E Lee was the most miserable man God ever bred...

Opposite: "No rest" was an appropriate way to describe an exhausted-looking Ozzy Osbourne in 1988: fat, forty and on the fags.

"If you're living with a miserable fucker who never speaks to you, it spreads through the band like a cancer. When you did a good gig with Jake, you thought you were going to fucking hang yourself."

Jake was less dramatic. Stating that he could no longer tolerate Ozzy's mood swings and the musical restrictions placed upon him, and confirming that his job had become an ordeal, he added: "I also became really disillusioned about the whole music business because of all the shitty things Ozzy said about me in the press."

Meanwhile, Dolores (Dee) Rhoads was being inundated with letters from fans eager to know if there were any plans to release live material featuring her son. She contacted Ozzy, and in May 1987, *Tribute* was released in honour of Randy Rhoads.

Recorded on tour in 1981 with the Ozzy/Rhoads/Sarzo/Aldridge line-up and including Don Airey on keyboards, this was an unusual live album for one reason: it sounded *great*. Serving as a showcase for Rhoads, it caught him at the peak of his playing, turning out the imaginative blend of power, precision, melody, speed, colour and intricacy that was his trademark. It reached number 13 in the charts in Britain and number six in the USA.

Describing *Tribute* as a "beautiful memory", Ozzy revealed that in planning the release with Sharon, he had insisted on only one thing: "Don't put it out at some ludicrous price and with a black album cover showing a guitar leaning against a tombstone."

With Soussan and Lee now out of the picture, Ozzy called Bob Daisley back to the fold, and recruited young guitar wizard Zakk Wylde, who had his own band, Pride And Glory.

Wylde had heard Ozzy mention on the Howard Stern show that he was looking for a guitarist, but didn't dream he might be eligible for the job himself. Later, a mutual photographer friend offered to pass a tape to Ozzy, and Zakk was invited to audition. His arrival brought a new enthusiasm and sense of purpose to the group, and keyboardist John Sinclair, who set about *No Rest For The Wicked* with gusto.

If Ozzy had tested his supporters' loyalties with *Bark At The Moon* and especially *The Ultimate Sin*, this was their reward. The new album marked a convincing return to form: passionately heavy, it offered a deafening alternative to the glam-rock outfits such as Poison and Guns N' Roses who were packing the stadiums. Released in October 1988, it charted at number 23 in the UK and number 13 in the US.

Ozzy crowed: "Zakk's everything I've been looking for: he's got a great personality, he's dedicated to his instrument and he's just wonderful to have around cos he's always up – he's never down. In rehearsals and that, he'll tell me off sometimes and make me do things, which is just great – he's so different to Jake, who never said anything to anybody... We all communicate like a family and Zakk's only 21, he's brilliant and, let's face it, he'll only get better."

MIRACLE MAN

It was long overdue. Ozzy had been castigated for years by American TV evangelists accusing him of being a Satanist. A rabble-rousing, money-grabbing breed, the preachers were often unmasked as worse sinners than their flocks, and hypocrites to boot.

Like his heroes The Beatles before him, Ozzy saw his albums being destroyed in ritual burnings, *Speak Of The Devil* (the American title) being one which was hurled on the bonfire. He was banned from concert-halls and whole towns, and when he did play, religious fundamentalists would turn up at venues to leaflet the audiences.

A leading Catholic, Cardinal John O'Connor, one-time Archbishop of New York, warned the world that Ozzy was hell's own messenger. One TV evangelist and Ozzy opponent, Oral Roberts, appealed to viewers for $7 million, claiming that God would literally strike him dead if he failed to meet his financial target. Ozzy sent him a dollar – explaining that it should go towards his psychiatric bill.

Then there was Jimmy Swaggart, perhaps the most famous of them all. Keen to denounce Ozzy as a devil's disciple and a parent's nightmare, Swaggart fell from grace spectacularly when he was caught in a hotel with a prostitute. The moral majority was not impressed, despite his tearful, televised pleas to God for forgiveness.

In "Miracle Man", Ozzy takes his revenge on Jimmy Swaggart: "Now Jimmy, he got busted with his pants down/Repent ye wretched sinner, self-righteous clown..."

The first track on the album, it finds Ozzy back on top of things, fully engaged, as Wylde's riff blares out, loud and proud, amid charging tempos.

DEVIL'S DAUGHTER

Ozzy was at it again. "I'll feel your creeping flesh if you're to be possessed/Then I will desecrate what you've become..."

It would be lovely to think that this was intended as an extra "fuck you" to Swaggart, but whatever, the evil aura is compounded by a stuttering vocal with a darkly compelling melodic hook.

"I think that this LP, more than any, has the root of Sabbath in it," explained Ozzy. "And, of course, I think this album's great. I had fun making it, I really did." With "Devil's Daughter", a fired-up rhythm section and a high-powered chorus keep the energy levels of "Miracle Man" cracking on, while the flamboyant lead guitar and robust rhythm play bear out the first impressions: Zakk Wylde was a Good Thing.

A musician with special interests in Southern-fried boogie and country rock as well as heavy metal, he took to his new guitar-hero role intuitively. "As far as me and Zakk are concerned, I'm proud to have discovered a new talent," declared Ozzy. "The most rewarding thing is remembering this raggedy-arsed kid walking through the door and ultimately becoming this great guy. And Zakk Wylde is a great fucking guy!"

He added: "You need young guys – why should I want old farts around me? I'm old enough. But having young guys in the band keeps me young. It keeps me in touch with what the kids are about... I'd much rather have young musicians with me than when you look to the back of the stage and see all those bald patches... and the older generation don't buy the records like the younger kids do."

Ozzy realized how easily he could intimidate his more junior recruits: "For the first month, it's very hard for new guys because they all believe what they've read in the papers. They think I'm a lunatic with an axe who runs around chopping people's heads off all day. I'm not like that at all!"

BLOODBATH IN PARADISE

On the evening of August 9, 1969, a band of disciples of insane cult leader Charles Manson went to a house at 10050 Cielo Drive, Beverly Hills, and murdered all the occupants. The assassins – three women and a man – knew who lived at the address, but that wasn't

"HAVING YOUNG GUYS IN THE BAND KEEPS ME YOUNG. IT KEEPS ME IN TOUCH WITH WHAT THE KIDS ARE ABOUT..."

Ozzy Osbourne

important. They selected the mansion because it was isolated. Their frenzied attacks left four victims with 102 stab wounds; the fifth victim was shot.

Sharon Tate, who was eight months pregnant and shared the home with her lover, film director Roman Polanski, was tied up and slaughtered in the living room, as was the internationally successful hair stylist Jay Sebring. Outside, coffee heiress Abigail Folger and her boyfriend Voytek Frykowski were slumped on the ground, alongside the body of Steve Parent, a young man who had arrived in his car to visit the caretaker. He was gunned down with a .22 calibre pistol. Jay Sebring and Voytek Frykowski were shot too. Parent and Frykowski were also bludgeoned around the head. On a door, the word "pig" was written in blood.

After midnight, the Manson Family members set out again, this time with their leader. They arrived at 3301 Waverly Drive and butchered husband and wife Leno and Rosemary LaBianca, stabbing them a total of 67 times, carving the word "war" into Leno's stomach. More slogans were daubed in blood around the house – "death to pigs" and "rise". Infamously, the mis-spelt "healther skelter" glared violently from the fridge door.

The atrocities which shocked America have been revisited in songs ever since, and this is Ozzy's.

"Can you hear them in the darkness?/Helter skelter, spiral madness (yeah)", torments the singer, returning Manson and his sidekicks to a decent society where they can again cause carnage and terror – in our nightmares. Not content with reintroducing Manson as a modern-day bogeyman, Ozzy added a mischievous touch: a backwards-playing message.

He revealed: "You know on the beginning of "Blood Bath In Paradise" – all those weird noises and that weird talking? That's all a big joke. If you play it backwards, it says, 'Your mother sells whelks in Hull'. I'm still waiting for some dickhead to pick up on that and tell people I'm sending messages to the Devil." Some dickhead undoubtedly did.

Meanwhile, Ozzy was inviting trouble with the video for another album track, "Crazy Babies", a song about children born to mothers on crack. It was banned.

"There must be some sick people working for these censorship boards," he raved. "They must be a bunch of perverts to read anything into that video. It makes me sick. I mean, if I had a pair of tits and my name was Madonna, they wouldn't have blinked an eye."

He whizzed on: "I could release a version of "My Way" and somebody in America would find something to read into it, something disgusting." Ozzy concluded: "It's not me you have to worry about. It's all of them – the PMRC who try to ban the shows and the fucking sheriff in Texas who says he can't guarantee my safety if I show my face in town. These are the people that cause all the trouble in America. I don't have to lift a finger."

DEMON ALCOHOL

Ozzy was struggling with his addictions to drink and drugs. By now, he was able to admit freely that he had a problem, but despite his valiant attempts to clean up and dry out, he was still a few years away from winning the war.

"Demon Alcohol" – a song that sounds as tough as Ozzy's drinking capacity – was and remains a warning, a testament to the seductiveness of booze. It's definitely Ozzy's song, whether or not Bob Daisley wrote or co-wrote the words.

"I'll watch you lose control, consume your very soul," says the bottle to the singer, later referring back to the controversial Blizzard Of Ozz track: "Don't speak of suicide solutions, you took my hand, I'm here to stay".

Ozzy's public stance on drinking had changed over the years. Once, he was challenging: "I get high. I get fucked up. What the hell's wrong with getting fucked up?"

But now he was facing the fact that things had gone too far, stating in true AA style: "All I know is, I am an alcoholic and my name is Ozzy. And I've gotta take certain steps to try and arrest the disease. Because I'm either gonna kill myself, kill someone else or I'm gonna go insane... It's got to the point now where I don't get happy-pissed, I go bulldozing around. I don't even know what I'm doing or where I'm at. Sharon says she's terrified when she sees me drink now. It upsets the whole family, close friends and everybody that works for me."

He added: "I've fucked up so many things through drugs and drink... I was like a mad dog chasing my tail... I've polluted every cell in my body with this crap, so my body gets pissed off when it can't get it."

Ozzy confided that he'd become "a fit-drinker", going into spasms during withdrawal, which is why he had originally sought proper detox treatment at the Betty Ford clinic and had joined AA to try and control his desires. One popular story insists that on his first visit to Betty Ford's, Ozzy believed he was going there to learn to drink in moderation – and immediately checked out on discovering that there was no bar.

"I met Betty Ford a couple of times," he remembered later. "She was a very quiet lady. She'd come in like royalty, have the unit polished. She was all right, though. She'd hover like a blow-up doll at one end of the wing and then go out the other. It was, like, 13 Hail Bettys and she'd go home."

Finally: "You name it, I drank it, from whisky to gin and cider. I didn't care if I lived or died."

Other tracks on the album are the rocking fan favourite "Crazy Babies"; "Breaking All The Rules", an incitement to have the courage of your convictions; "Fire In The Sky" (hopefully not a Deep Purple reference!), which emerges from an atmospheric synth intro to explore the effects of childhood trauma upon the grown adult; the infectious "Tattooed Dancer", introducing the dominating, "mean, hard woman" who knows what she wants; and the hidden bonus track, "Hero".

THE 1990S

THE MORE THINGS CHANGE, THE MORE THEY STAY THE SAME. IN THE
EARLY 90S, RONNIE JAMES DIO REJOINED BLACK SABBATH. AGAIN,
A MESSY SPLIT ENSUED. AND IN 1997, IT WAS OZZY WHO RETURNED.
THE ORIGINAL BLACK SABBATH – "THE TRUE GODS OF METAL," AS
METALLICA'S LARS ULRICH CALLED THEM – WERE AT LAST REUNITED.

Between 1987 and 1995, Tony Martin recorded five albums with Black Sabbath. The only singer who has made more albums with the band is Ozzy.

Martin did a job for Tony Iommi when Sabbath's career was at its lowest ebb. If he lacked the star quality of his famous predecessors – Ozzy, Dio, Ian Gillan and Glenn Hughes – Martin was a solid performer and a reliable foil for Iommi when the guitarist most needed it.

And yet, the three albums that Sabbath made with Martin in the 90s – *Tyr, Cross Purposes* and *Forbidden* – were overshadowed by much bigger events: the reunions with Ronnie James Dio and Ozzy.

It was in 1991, after Geezer Butler rejoined Black Sabbath, that Dio followed suit. The last man in was Vinny Appice – completing the line-up that had recorded *Mob Rules* in 1981. A new album, *Dehumanizer*, was released in June 1992, when Sabbath also began a world tour in Brazil.

In the same month, coincidentally, Ozzy set off on a tour that that was billed as his last – titled No More Tours, after his 1991 album *No More*

Tears. The album had been another huge hit, but after so many years on the road, Ozzy felt that enough was enough. He also wanted to finish on a high. For his final bow – two nights at the Pacific Amphitheater in Costa Mesa, California on November 14 and 15, 1992 – Ozzy invited Black Sabbath to be part of the event. The offer was for Sabbath, with Dio, to perform as the opening act, and then for the original Sabbath line-up, with Ozzy and Bill Ward, to reunite for the encore.

Iommi and Butler accepted, but Dio was outraged. Ever since he had first replaced Ozzy in Black Sabbath in 1979, there had been a fierce rivalry between the two men. Dio flatly refused to do the Costa Mesa shows. He told Iommi: "I'm not supporting a clown. Sorry, I have more pride than that."

Iommi knew that Dio would not back down. He also knew that this was the end of the line for Dio and Sabbath. On November 13, Ronnie James Dio sang on stage with Black Sabbath for the last time at the Kaiser Convention Center in Oakland, California.

The following night, Sabbath opened for Ozzy in Costa Mesa with Rob Halford of Judas Priest as their singer. After only two days of rehearsals with Sabbath in the week before the gigs, Halford performed heroically on a selection of songs from the Ozzy and Dio eras. And the grand finale for the second show saw the original band playing together for the first time since Live Aid. They did four songs: 'Black Sabbath', 'Fairies Wear Boots', 'Iron Man' and 'Paranoid'. "It was," Iommi said, "a great thing to do."

There were conversations about a full-scale reunion, but with Ozzy considering himself semi-retired, the plans were soon abandoned. Instead, Iommi and Butler brought Tony Martin back into the band for a new Sabbath album, *Cross Purposes*, released in 1994. Butler exited again before the 1995 album *Forbidden* – a misguided attempt to update Sabbath's sound, which resulted in abject failure. Iommi promptly dissolved the band.

Ozzy's retirement would prove short-lived. In 1995 came a new solo album, *Ozzmosis*, and the jokingly named Retirement Sucks tour. In 1996, he headlined Ozzfest, his very own bespoke heavy metal festival – a two-day event featuring a bunch of Sabbath-worshipping support acts, including Slayer, Danzig and Sepultura. And it was for the following year's Ozzfest that Ozzy and Black Sabbath were reunited.

At this time, Bill Ward was unable to participate due to ill health. In his place was Mike Bordin, formerly of Faith No More, who was then a member of Ozzy's band. Even so, this reunion was a bigger deal than the one-offs at Live Aid and Costa Mesa. Ozzfest was expanded in 1997 –

rolled out into 28 cities across the US. Ozzy had a dual role, performing with his own band before closing the shows with Sabbath. The tour was a huge success. And at the end of that year, Bill was back for two homecoming shows at Birmingham's NEC on December 4 and 5.

For the band, and for the fans that had waited so long to see the original Black Sabbath on a British stage once again, it was a momentous and emotional occasion. As Ozzy said: "The Birmingham shows were two of the most memorable gigs I've ever done in my life."

Ward's health would remain an issue. In 1998, during rehearsals for a European tour, he suffered a heart attack. While he was recovering, Vinny Appice acted as stand-in. Appice stayed on as part of the entourage, in case of emergency, when Ward returned for the Reunion tour in 1999. But Ward got through the whole tour, and played brilliantly throughout.

Another turbulent decade in the history of Black Sabbath ended on a triumphant note. Bill Ward said in 1999: "I think we're playing better now than years ago." Ozzy agreed. "I don't know what the fucking chemistry is," he said, "but we've got it." And for Ozzy, that chemistry extended beyond music. He said simply: "Tony and Geezer and Bill are my oldest, dearest friends."

Opposite: The second of three successful outings for Ronnie James Dio and Black Sabbath came with the *Dehumanizer* album in 1992.

Above: Skinny, sober and successful, Ozzy rejoined his mates Geezer and Tony for the Ozzfest in 1997. Bill Ward, sidelined by ill-health, was absent.

TYR / DEHUMANIZER
(1990 / 1992)

WHEN THE FIRST BLACK SABBATH ALBUM OF THE 1990S DIED A QUIET
DEATH, TONY IOMMI KNEW THAT DRASTIC ACTION WAS REQUIRED.
WITH HIS TRUSTY LIEUTENANT GEEZER BUTLER AS CATALYST, A
REUNION WITH RONNIE JAMES DIO FOLLOWED... ONLY FOR DIO TO
QUIT AGAIN WHEN HIS NEMESIS CAME BACK TO HAUNT HIM.

At the turn of the 90s, Black Sabbath, the band that had defined heavy metal, was being outgunned by a new generation of metal bands. These were the very people that had grown up listening to Sabbath albums: Metallica, Slayer, Pantera. Alternative rock stars Faith No More had covered 'War Pigs' on their breakthrough 1989 album *The Real Thing*. Guns N' Roses had stolen the riff to Sabbath's 'Zero The Hero' for the song 'Paradise City', from their multi-million selling album *Appetite For Destruction*.

Sabbath, meanwhile, couldn't get arrested in 1990. Tony Iommi had felt as if the band had "turned a corner" with the *Headless Cross* album in 1989, but the follow-up, named *Tyr*, failed to break the Top 200 in the US. The album, inspired in part by Norse mythology, included some strong tracks, such as 'Anno Mundi', 'The Sabbath Stones' and 'The Law Maker'. Iommi describe its failure with characteristic understatement: "Disheartening."

At the end of that year, Iommi's spirits were lifted by the return of Geezer Butler to Black Sabbath. On September 8, 1990, Butler had joined Sabbath on stage at London's Hammersmith Odeon for an encore – playing on two songs, 'Children Of The Grave' and 'Iron Man'. Iommi enjoyed having his old friend up there with him. Butler enjoyed it so much that he accepted Iommi's invitation to rejoin the band in place of Neil Murray.

A few months later, Butler attended a Dio concert and ended up jamming with them on 'Neon Knights'. He told Iommi that it felt great to be on stage with Ronnie again. The wheels had been set in motion.

At this time, Dio was very much open to a Sabbath reunion. He had been successful with his own band in the decade since he resigned from Sabbath over the *Live Evil* debacle, but Dio's most recent album *Lock Up The Wolves* had, like *Tyr*, flopped. It was 1979 all over again: Black Sabbath and Ronnie James Dio needed each other.

Before a formal offer was made to Dio, rehearsals for a new Sabbath album had already begun, with Tony Martin on vocals and Cozy Powell on drums. Iommi's first task was an unpleasant one – firing Tony

Martin. "It wasn't really fair on him," Iommi later admitted. He then had to mediate between Dio and Cozy, who had never much liked each other when they were members of Rainbow in the late 70s.

Dio suggested a new drummer for Sabbath – Simon Wright, who had replaced Vinny Appice for Dio's *Lock Up The Wolves*, and had previously played for seven years with AC/DC. Iommi insisted on Cozy, with predictable results. As the band worked on new songs, the relationship between singer and drummer went from bad to worse. At one point, Cozy warned Iommi: "If that little cunt says anything to me, I'm going to smash him in the face!" In the end, it didn't come to that.

What followed was yet another comical episode in the story of Black Sabbath. For a brief period, Dio went back to his home in LA to consider his options. In the meantime, Iommi brought Tony Martin back, so that work on the album could continue – only for Dio to return, leaving Iommi to break the news to Martin that he was out again. Then, a bizarre denouement: on a day off, Cozy Powell was out riding his horse when it had a heart attack and fell on him. Cozy sustained a broken hip and was forced to withdraw from Black Sabbath. The door was open for Vinny Appice to return.

After a year in the making, the new Sabbath album, *Dehumanizer*, was finally completed in early 1992 at Rockfield Studios in Wales with producer Reinhold Mack, famed for his work with Queen in the early 80s. Released on June 22, the album had, in flashes, some of the magic of *Heaven And Hell* and *Mob Rules*. Two standout tracks, 'Time Machine' and 'I', were the best that Sabbath had recorded since Dio had last been in the band. *Dehumanizer* also returned Black Sabbath to the US Top 50 – still a long way short of the band's early 70s peak, but a huge improvement upon recent years.

And yet, within six months of the album's release, Dio was gone again. When Iommi first informed Dio of the Costa Mesa gigs with Ozzy, he

Opposite: Tony Iommi on stage in Seville, Spain in 1991.

knew what the reply would be. Dio knew that Ozzy was the original and true voice of Black Sabbath – and didn't try to deny it. What he could not accept was the indignity, as he saw it, of being Ozzy's support act. His pride would not allow it.

At the end of 1992, Tony Iommi was hoping to reunite the original Black Sabbath. This would happen, eventually. Before that, however, Iommi would have to endure the darkest days of Sabbath's entire career.

NO MORE TEARS
(1991)

AT THE END OF 1988, OZZY SET OUT ON THE ROAD TO PROMOTE
NO REST FOR THE WICKED WITH A FAMILIAR FIGURE ON BASS.
BLACK SABBATH'S GEEZER BUTLER STEPPED IN FOR THE TOUR
(COMMEMORATED ON THE LIVE MINI-ALBUM, *JUST SAY OZZY*, WHICH
WAS RELEASED TO LITTLE ACCLAIM IN FEBRUARY 1990).

Ozzy's on-off efforts to quit booze and drugs were definitely off again. By the time the band stepped on to a plane at Newark bound for the Moscow Music Peace Festival in 1989, Ozzy was tired and emotional... and in need of the toilet.

He was billed alongside Bon Jovi, Mötley Crüe, Skid Row, Cinderella, The Scorpions and Gorky Park for the Soviet Union's first major rock concert by Western artists.

The extravaganza, held in August in the Lenin Stadium, was staged by the Make A Difference Foundation, who, in conjunction with producers and organizers in the US and the USSR, were promoting international co-operation on fighting drug abuse among young people.

Journalist Adam Curry was on the flight with all of the artists. He wrote: "Ozzy was totally hammered... So I'm sitting with Geezer, shooting the Sabbath shit, when Ozzy starts mumbling loudly near the rear bulkhead."

The girlfriend of Bon Jovi drummer Tico Torres was in the toilet – and Ozzy couldn't or wouldn't wait his turn.

"I looked up to see Ozzy standing spreadeagled in the aisle, with a huge, dark spot in his crotch area and a growing pool of urine at his feet," wrote Curry. "What was funny was how both Sharon and Geezer acted as if they witnessed this type of behaviour daily. Sharon even had a change of clothes for Ozzy in her carry-on."

Ozzy was infamous for his spontaneous leaks – the Alamo simply being the most controversial. He had also showered Hitler's memorial in Berlin, had relieved himself out of a venue window not realizing that fans were queuing just below, and had been interviewed by the FBI over rumours that he intended to pee on the steps of the White House.

Sharon was indeed used to all this, turning a blind eye to Ozzy's "idiosyncrasies" while ruling his career with a rod of iron. She had often supported her husband's more outrageous antics because of their publicity value, and had been suspected by many of orchestrating the incident where he bit the head off a dove in the offices of CBS/Epic Records.

Yet, she could be formidable if she thought things had gone too far. There are stories of Sharon punching groupies and fighting Ozzy with her bare fists or any other handy object as she struggled to keep him away from cocaine. It seemed that she was coming out on top.

In 1988, Ozzy had said: "I'm John Osbourne now... You've got no fear of me being fucking Ozzy Osbourne around here – because if I am, Sharon goes, 'Fuck off. Go and soak your head in the horse trough and don't come back until you've found your brains.'"

But shortly after the Moscow festival – on September 2, 1989 – Ozzy started drinking heavily at home, flew into a violent rage and tried to strangle Sharon while snarling a warning: "We've decided that you've got to go." She hit the panic button.

What started as a family celebration for daughter Aimee's sixth birthday ended with Ozzy being frog-marched off by the police and charged with attempted murder.

He said: "I mixed some medication I'd been prescribed by a psychiatrist with alcohol and I just blacked out. I woke up the next day in Amersham police station, and I honestly didn't know what was going on. The copper said, 'Do you know why you're here?' and they told me I'd threatened to kill my wife." He also admitted: "I don't remember anything. I was *gone*. I went to court and everything, but she dropped the charges."

Pleading temporary insanity, Ozzy – horrified by what he had done – was ordered by the court to go into rehab at Huntercombe Manor, in England. He spent three months there.

"But I came out, I drank again, I couldn't stop... I was a mess." Finally, said Ozzy, "All that craziness stopped once I put the cork back into the bottle."

Ozzy entered the Nineties on Prozac and an exercise bike, and with a new, healthy diet – no red meat, no raw animals. Then he went back to work.

Opposite: Fitter, happier – but still haunted by his demons: Ozzy Osbourne smartened up his act in the late 1990s.

No More Tears is often described as Ozzy's first sober album, and it has been hailed as one of his finest. A mixture of ballads and pounding rockers of consistently high quality, it's an album he made to satisfy himself and nobody else.

Pre-production work began with Zakk Wylde, Randy Castillo and bass player Mike Inez (later to join Alice In Chains), who initiated the title track. Legendary Motörhead mainman Lemmy helped out with the lyrics for "I Don't Want To Change The World", "Desire" and "Hellraiser" and wrote all the words for "Mama, I'm Coming Home."

When it came to recording time, Bob Daisley's phone rang. "Mike was Ozzy's bass player at the time," Daisley told Jeb Wright. "I got a call from Ozzy and he said he was having problems getting the songs recorded and he asked me to come down and give it a try. I played on the whole album. Mike Inez got credit as playing some bass on it but he didn't do any of it... I had great fun doing it. I got involved with the lyrics, but they didn't use them. They used my lyrics to inspire other lyrics to be written... I just played on that one." It was Daisley's last work on an Ozzy album.

The album was released in October 1991. It charted at number 17 in the UK and was a resounding number seven hit in the US.

Everything was looking up for the cleaned-up, slimmed-down Ozzy Osbourne. And then, perversely, he announced his retirement – and a No More Tours tour.

MR TINKERTRAIN

Kicking off the album in controversial style, "Mr Tinkertrain" adopts the creepy persona of a paedophile who abducts a young child: "I've got the kind of toys you've never seen... Little angel, come and sit upon my knee."

"Fuck knows where that came from," commented Daisley.

Naturally, Ozzy came in for some flak, not just for tackling a taboo subject in the first place but also for the song's explicit depiction of an imaginary scenario involving the man and his victim.

There were, however, some very unexpected reactions, with one reviewer describing it as a "fun song" with "comedic" lyrics, a classic example of Ozzy's "humorous side".

Generally, listeners took the view that the language was too simplistic and the vision too narrow to make anything other than the most banal protest against child abuse.

Lyrics apart, "Mr Tinkertrain" is a storming rock track, Zakk Wylde riffing madly as if briefly consumed by the spirit of AC/DC. Wylde enjoyed the recording sessions enormously, having gained in confidence

Above: Hollywood's Walk Of Fame received three of Black Sabbath's four hand prints in 1992. Who would have thought the kids from Aston would come this far?

Opposite: Ever the showman, Ozzy's style continued to be as distinctive and idiosyncratic as ever during the 1990s.

and capability. He confided to writer Gary Graff: "On the first album [*No Rest For The Wicked*]... Ozzy didn't even know if I could cut it. He was more or less constantly over my shoulder going, 'This sounds like Jimi Hendrix, don't do that,' or, 'Zakk, just sound like yourself.' But at the time I didn't even know who the fuck I was or what my fucking sound was. I knew I liked playing Les Pauls through Marshall amps and playing pentatonic scales."

By the time of *No More Tears*, Wylde said, "I had done a record, done a tour and I was happy with the songs we had. So it was more relaxed. Ozzy felt it too; he gave me more freedom that time out."

I DON'T WANT TO CHANGE THE WORLD

Ozzy: "I won a Grammy for this one. The song's meaning is self-explanatory, in respect that lines like, 'Tell me I'm a sinner, I've got news for you'... well, it's kind of a spoof on me, you know."

A smart retort to the enemy – any enemy – the track picks up and runs with the vigorous rockability of "Mr Tinkertrain". Co-written by Lemmy, Ozzy, Wylde and Castillo, it was awarded a Grammy in 1993 for Best Metal Performance.

According to Zakk Wylde, the band knew they were on to a good thing in the studio, but they didn't know how good. They could not have realized that they were producing Grammy-quality material, or that the album would be such a hit in the US.

Wylde told Gary Graff: "It's like a Salvador Dali painting. He didn't sit around and go, 'I'm gonna paint this today. It's gonna be my most famous one.' If he got inspired, he painted it. If we get inspired, we just write it and record it. You just get lucky, man."

The atmosphere in the sessions was certainly indicative of a band that were feeling happy and creative. Recording first at Bearsville Studios in New York and later relocating to LA, they exchanged a series of malodorous practical jokes instigated by Ozzy, who cracked a stink bomb in the room shared by Wylde and Castillo.

As the tit-for-tat continued, the stink bombs gave way to something altogether more solid and messy. "We had a blast when we were up there," chuckled Wylde.

Ozzy later paid an appropriate tribute to Lemmy, an old friend: "I always think of Lemmy when I see a can of Carlsberg Special... it's great stuff if you want a night out on the booze. The trick isn't to start early on in the evening with it, but later on when you're ready to collapse. You don't last very long with this stuff, it's so strong – and that's speaking from experience."

MAMA, I'M COMING HOME

Although it's generally accepted that Lemmy penned the lyrics, he did so expressly for the man who would sing them. The title comes from Ozzy's regular phone call home to "Mama", his pet name for Sharon, as the end of each tour drew near.

The sentiments of the song, in part, seem quite appropriate: "I've seen your face a hundred times/Every day we've been apart." In other lines, a fictitious element arises, with a submissive lover returning, tail between legs, to a lying, flint-hearted woman.

Clearly, this is no reflection of the relationship between Ozzy and Sharon which, despite its temptestuous rows, was and is based on real love, respect and teamwork, with each understanding and offering the qualities needed by the other.

"I WAS FRIGHTENED OF LIVING AND FRIGHTENED OF DYING."

Ozzy Osbourne

Musically, it's a dramatic and tuneful ballad which progresses from Wylde's acoustic picking and emphatic chording, to a spot of jamming and then a climactic finish built up by backing vocals. Bob Daisley singles it out as one which was "fun to do" on his fretless bass.

NO MORE TEARS

Reportedly recorded as a post-script to the sessions – as "Paranoid" had been – "No More Tears" was originally titled "Say Hello To Heaven". A portrait of a serial killer stalking prostitutes, it vividly describes the man in the dark, his parting kiss on the cold lips of a victim, and an additional twist of insanity: "I never wanted it to end this way my love, my darling/ Believe me when I say to you in love I think I'm falling here..."

The seven-minute musical adventure starts out with a bassline much beloved of Ozzy fans and carries on through a progression of sounds and styles that include a Beatles-flavoured middle section. A call-and-response exchange between Zakk's guitar and Ozzy's vocals is prominently featured, while synths, keyboards and a moody piano add to the atmospheric impact. And it rocks, too.

A real team effort credited to Ozzy, Wylde, Castillo, Michael Inez and co-producer John Purdell, it was one of those songs that sprang to life by accident – just like old times.

Zakk Wylde recalled: "Ozzy started singing the melody, and I just played that Tony Iommi-esque riff with the flat fives in there. I had my slide in my hand too, so I worked out some stuff with that."

Bob Daisley remembers that the song was a fait accompli by the time he arrived to take over the bass duties. He said: "Mike Inez used to come and watch me play in the studio. I found him to be a very friendly guy. Mike had the idea of starting the song with the bass and he had an intro that he had written. I changed it around a bit when I came in."

ZOMBIE STOMP

A song about the nature of addiction, "Zombie Stomp" sums up Ozzy's countless but finally successful efforts to quit his vices.

"Hey, hey, do the zombie stomp/Thinkin' how it could have been if I had never let them in..."

Said Ozzy: "For many years I was trying to stop the booze and I couldn't stop it, man, it was like a monkey on my back. I'm not one of those holier-than-thou fuckers either. Believe me, if I thought I could successfully go to the fridge and get a can of beer and have a good old fucking laugh, then I would. But I know if I go to that beer then I'm fucking over. One's too many and ten's not enough."

He has also insisted: "There's not enough alcohol in the world for me. There's no such thing as moderation in Ozzy Osbourne's vocabulary... It's all or nothing – whether it's drugs, sex, drink, falling in love, anything."

He wasn't joking: "Back then it was two cases of Dom Perignon, a case of Hennessey... beer, drugs, everything. I was doing four bottles of brandy a day and as much cocaine, pot and champagne as I could handle. I was out of control." That was as well as the morphine, Demerol, Valium, barbiturates and steroids.

"Everyone blames rock'n'roll for their problems," reflected Ozzy. "But let me tell you the truth. It's a great way to make a living. But if you want to be an idiot and take bags of drugs and drink, you will die. I've tried the lot and I'm not proud of it."

He saw tragedy strike down his friends and colleagues: "It was terribly sad so many stars died, just for the sake of silliness. I'm no better than John Bonham or Keith Moon, just luckier."

Then there was Def Leppard's Steve Clark: "He didn't drink for pleasure. He drank to escape. He had too much too soon and couldn't cope. He had it all – talent, nice houses and cars. Now he's dead at 30."

"A lot of my drinking friends died in their forties – heart attacks," Ozzy expanded. "One guy's liver exploded. There but for the grace of God go I. There must be a guiding star over me."

Ozzy's efforts to get on the wagon and stay there would invariably come to grief when touring time rolled around again, with the easily obtained drugs and drinks holding out the offer of some fun, some familiarity, a sense of camaraderie and a relief from the pressures, the relentless grind of travelling and the boring hours spent just hanging around.

In the end, it was not the attack on Sharon, or the deaths of his friends, that saw Ozzy sober up; it was a moment of personal realization.

He said: "I just couldn't stand it any more – the shakes, the horrors, the phone ringing thinking, 'Fuck, it's bad news,' and that horrible feeling of blacking out..."

He added: "I was frightened of living and frightened of dying, and that's a horrible place to be. I just didn't have the bottle to end it. I'd wake up in the morning and if I didn't have anything to worry about, I'd worry. And it would escalate into this incredible dark monster in my head, and the only escape I used to know was drugs and booze."

Told by a psychiatrist that he had a chemical imbalance in the brain caused by his over-indulgences, Ozzy was put on the anti-depressant Prozac and prescribed anti-seizure medication. He's resigned to the fact that he'll have to keep on taking the tablets, struggling with the demons and, probably, visiting his therapist for the rest of his life.

Other tracks on the album are the tough "Desire", a commitment to keep on rocking; the heavy-duty "SIN" (Shadows In The Night), which opens, in archetypal Ozzy style, with the words: "A psycho driver twisted in my head/Silence broken, but there's nothing said"; the rollicking "Hellraiser", pouring out clichés about the heroic rock'n'roller on the "endless road"; "Time After Time", a love-lorn softie; the hard and heavy "AVH", apparently an abbreviation for Aston Villa Highway and not the rumoured "alcohol, valium and hash", despite the suggestions of its lyrics; and the country-coloured "Road To Nowhere", the third and final ballad which would seem to look back on Ozzy's life. The remastered version of the album includes two extra tracks – "Don't Blame Me", the B-side of the "Mama, I'm Coming Home" single, and "Party With the Animals", from the soundtrack to "Buffy The Vampire Slayer".

Tracks on the preceding mini-album, *Just Say Ozzy*, are "Miracle Man", "Bloodbath In Paradise", "Shot In The Dark", "Tattooed Dancer", "Sweet Leaf" and "War Pigs".

Opposite: Even during a particularly turbulent, and at times depressing, time in his life, Ozzy remained an engrossing subject for photographers. Even in his lowest moments, that old electric personality shone through.

CROSS PURPOSES / FORBIDDEN
(1994 / 1995)

AFTER THE FOUR FOUNDING MEMBERS OF BLACK SABBATH REGROUPED FOR
OZZY'S "FAREWELL" IN 1992, THERE WERE PLANS FOR A MORE PERMANENT
REUNION. WHEN THIS FAILED TO MATERIALIZE, TONY MARTIN WAS REINSTATED
AS SABBATH SINGER. TWO ALBUMS FOLLOWED: THE SECOND A DISASTER. AND
IN 1995, A DISCONSOLATE TONY IOMMI WALKED AWAY FROM BLACK SABBATH.

According to Geezer Butler, the Black Sabbath album released in 1994, *Cross Purposes*, started out as something altogether different. Not a Sabbath album at all, but a side project led by him and Tony Iommi.

"That was the time," Butler said, "when the original band were talking about getting back together for a reunion tour. Tony and myself just went in with a couple of people, did an album. It was like an Iommi/Butler project album."

Instead, it ended up as a Black Sabbath album – primarily, because it featured not only Iommi and Butler but also Tony Martin and Geoff Nicholls. There was one new face, American drummer Bobby Rondinelli, a replacement for Vinny Appice, who had exited with Ronnie James Dio to make a new Dio album, *Strange Highways*. Rondinelli had a history in common with three other former members of Sabbath. Like Dio, Bob Daisley and Cozy Powell before him, he had previously starred in Rainbow.

Iommi said that he never considered singers other than Martin. It was in some way a reward for the loyal service that Martin had given to Sabbath. Iommi felt that he owed him another chance after dumping him twice during the making of *Dehumanizer*. Moreover, he knew what he was getting with Tony Martin, a singer who knew the band inside out.

Cross Purposes was recorded in the summer of 1993 at Monnow Valley Studios in Wales. The producer of the album, Leif Mases, had worked with Sabbath on the original recording of the song 'Time Machine', a version that was used on the soundtrack to the hit movie *Wayne's World*. To Iommi's amusement, Mases had also worked in the past with his fellow Swedes ABBA.

A surprise contributor to the album was Eddie Van Halen. He and Iommi had bonded back in 1978 when Van Halen toured with Sabbath. "Eddie became a great friend of mine on that tour," Iommi said. In 1993, Van Halen were touring the UK while Sabbath were rehearsing their album. Eddie jammed with them for an afternoon, in which they wrote a song together named 'Evil Eye'. The track, featuring a solo

from Eddie, was recorded – but on a small tape machine that Iommi used for basic demos. The poor quality of the recording meant that the original track could not be included on the album. It was later re-recorded by Sabbath alone. In addition, Eddie was not credited as a co-writer because he was under contract with Van Halen's record company Warner Brothers.

Cross Purposes was a solid album. The strongest track, 'Virtual Death', was formed around a colossal riff that was classic Iommi. But the reviews were not kind. American music magazine *Blender* dismissed the album as a "by-the-numbers potboiler". And after the relative success of *Dehumanizer*, sales dropped off again. On the US chart, *Cross Purposes* peaked at Number 122.

Following a European tour, Bobby Rondinelli was let go as Bill Ward made a brief comeback for a series of shows in South America with Kiss and Slayer. As Iommi had expected, Bill departed after those gigs. The real shock came when Geezer left again for Ozzy's band. Iommi responded by bringing back Cozy Powell and Neil Murray for a new Sabbath album. He also bowed to pressure from the band's record company to enlist a producer who would give a more contemporary edge to the album. "They said it would give us a bit more street cred," Iommi recalled. In fact, it would have the opposite effect.

The producer chosen was Ernie Cunnigan, better known as Ernie C, guitarist for Body Count, the rap-metal band led by hip-hop legend Ice-T. Certainly, Body Count's work had "street cred" – most notably, the song 'Cop Killer', which had created huge controversy in 1992. However, as producer for Black Sabbath, Cunnigan didn't have a clue.

The resulting album, titled *Forbidden*, was in Iommi's words "a total shambles". Due to Cunnigan's tin ear, Sabbath ended up sounding like a garage band, and a bad one at that. The album's opening track 'The Illusion Of Power', featuring a rap from Ice-T, merely proved that Black Sabbath and hip-hop were like oil and water.

Released on June 8, 1995, *Forbidden* was roundly panned in the rock press. It remains, by some distance, Black Sabbath's worst album. In the UK, it peaked at Number 71. In the US it did not even chart. On the subsequent tour, Cozy Powell quit and Bobby Rondinelli returned in his place. And in November 1995, the tour was cut short due to poor ticket sales. At this point, Iommi gave up fighting a losing battle. He broke up the band.

For Tony Iommi and Black Sabbath, the mid-90s were tough times. It was only when the reunion with Ozzy finally happened, in 1997, that this legendary band was restored to its former glory.

Opposite: Geezer Butler on Sabbath's Cross Purposes tour, Hammersmith Apollo, London, 1994. After this tour, Butler quit the band again.

Above: Sabbath on the Cross Purposes tour. Their next tour, in 1995, would be cancelled due to low ticket sales – at which point, even Tony Iommi gave up on the band.

OZZMOSIS
(1995)

THERE WERE THOSE WHO THOUGHT THAT OZZY'S "RETIREMENT" WOULD NEVER LAST. AND
THERE WERE THOSE WHO THOUGHT HE NEVER MEANT IT IN THE FIRST PLACE, THAT IT WAS A
PLOY TO SELL MORE ALBUMS AND TOUR TICKETS. THIS VIEWPOINT WAS REINFORCED ON THE
FINAL NIGHT OF THE NO MORE TOURS TOUR, AT COSTA MESA, CALIFORNIA IN NOVEMBER 1992.
CLIMAXING WITH A FOUR-SONG BLACK SABBATH REUNION, THE GIG ENDED WITH A SPECTACULAR
FIREWORKS DISPLAY WHICH REPORTEDLY SPELT OUT THE MESSAGE, "I'LL BE BACK."

Despite this, Ozzy seemed initially genuine in his desire to step out of public life. It was easier to avoid the temptations of drink and drugs when he was at home. He was becoming prone to illness and injury and was fed up with touring. And he wanted to spend time with Sharon and their three children, Aimee (born on September 2, 1983), Kelly (born October 27, 1984) and Jack (born November 8, 1985).

But Ozzy's idyllic vision of a future filled with domesticity and school sports days was bound to be short-lived.

"I went home, gained a stack of weight, bought motorcycles and guns and all this other shit," said Ozzy. "Then I started doing things I'd always wanted to do. I bought a football and played football with my son. I really enjoyed being a dad... for about a week. Then Sharon said to me one day, 'Is that it now? Are you finished?' She let me get all these things out of my system. Then she asked me what I wanted to do. And I said, 'I want to get a band, man.'" Ozzy was coming back.

"I never really went into retirement as such," he later confessed. "I mean, I'm always making these stupid, dumb fucking statements and then I wonder, 'What the fuck did I say that for?' I wanted to know what it was like to be off, not to be living on a schedule. I did the No More Tours tour and then I wondered, 'What the fuck do I do now? What is retirement?'"

During his absence, Ozzy had authorized the release of a double album, *Live and Loud*, recorded during the farewell tour with henchmen Wylde, Castillo and Inez. Issued in June 1993, it didn't bother the UK chart, although it reached a reasonable number 22 in the US.

Returning to the fray in 1994, Ozzy intended to make a fresh start with a new band, but there were lots of twists and turns before a line-up and production team was finally assembled.

The musicians originally answering his calls were guitarist Steve Vai, drummer Deen Castronovo and the reliable Bob Daisley. Ozzy and Vai wrote songs together and work began in Vai's LA studio before the singer decided that the partnership wasn't really working.

Ozzy said: "While Steve never treated me like anything less than a gentleman and I was fine with him, it was felt that maybe I should work with actual songwriters."

With Vai out of the picture, Ozzy recalled Zakk Wylde to the band. He also brought Geezer Butler in on bass. Bob Daisley said: "I thought, 'Oh fuck, thanks a lot.'"

The band that recorded the comeback album, *Ozzmosis* (originally titled *X-Ray*), comprised Wylde, Butler and Castronovo, with Rick Wakeman and producer Michael Beinhorn both contributing on keyboards. Beinhorn had been invited to replace *No More Tears* producers Duane Baron and John Purdell, who'd started work on the new album. Ozzy scrapped those recordings.

Ozzy had also been teaming up with various songwriters, first Mark Hudson and Steve Dudas, and then Jim Vallance. As a result, Ozzy had a whole host of co-writers for the album – Vai, Wylde, Purdell, Baron, Vallance, Hudson, Dudas, Butler and, on "See You On The Other Side", Lemmy.

Released in October 1995, *Ozzmosis* was an enormous hit in the US, peaking at number 4 (number 22 in the UK), but it doesn't sound quite as Ozzy had intended, which was "very fucking heavy".

Granted, it has heavy elements, but the keyboard arrangements and the ballads contribute to a more sophisticated result, and Ozzy himself later admitted to regretting the "sterile" sound.

Lyrically, there are some tender moments, but most of the tracks dwell on familiar topics, namely death and the afterlife. "Every time I try to get out of the darkness, it drags me back," sighed Ozzy.

The tour was called Retirement Sucks, and it hit the road without Zakk Wylde, who'd been in talks about a job with Guns N' Roses

Opposite: Ozzy's thousand-yard stare is interesting if you fancy a bit of amateur psychology; beneath it all, there's a scared little boy.

and wasn't sure if he'd be available. He agreed to give Ozzy his final decision on a certain date, but failed to call. Ozzy said: "All I wanted was a straight answer from him – but he didn't show me that respect."

Always on the lookout for a bright, new talent, Ozzy spotted a guitarist who "plays like a motherfucker". That was Joe Holmes. Holmes, who previously worked with Dave Lee Roth, was a pupil of Randy Rhoads. Rhoads, while on tour, would himself take classical guitar lessons, and would also arrange workshops in which he gave lessons to young players.

"It's really spooky," said Ozzy, "because when Joe plays the Randy Rhoads stuff, he plays just like him – it's like I can see Randy's fingers." He added: "I love giving guys a break and watching them develop. And they all develop, they all get egos, they all get pissed off and after that, they all fly from the nest. And then I get another one."

In a final line-up change, Geezer Butler left the tour half way through, suffering from homesickness, making way for Mike Inez to come back.

Ozzy and Sharon, meanwhile, were beginning to realize that they did not have to become slaves to the time-honoured album-tour-album-tour cycle. They were making plans for their own label, the short-lived Ozz Records, and for a heavy metal extravaganza they called the Ozzfest.

Ozzy said: "I was talking to Sharon... and she said that since radio and MTV had stopped playing our type of music, I, as one of the founding forefathers of what they call 'metal', should do something for the people that still like it."

It started as a two-day event in America in September 1996, with Ozzy headlining a bill that encompassed the best of the era's big bands including Slayer, Sepultura, Fear Factory and Biohazard and a spread of then up-and-coming acts such as Coal Chamber, Cellophane, Earth Crisis and Powerman 5000. Adding to the atmosphere was a variety of sideshows and booths for tattoos and body-piercing.

With 50,000 tickets sold across the two dates, the Ozzfest fulfilled it potential immediately. It would then mushroom into an annual, international touring package that would rehabilitate Ozzy as a major live attraction, a living legend, and a godfather and benefactor of heavy metal.

PERRY MASON

Information filtering out from the studio where Ozzy and the band were working "very, very hard" with producer Michael Beinhorn, said that the album would be unremittingly heavy.

"There's no turning back now," announced Ozzy. "I've lived with these songs for a long time. And if you think I'm bad now, wait until the mix, wait until the mastering! I'll wanna kill everybody!"

He also insisted: "No more "Goodbye To Romance" or "Mama, I'm Coming Home" – that's all fuckin' dead and history, man!" Eventually, the brief did widen, and the album was completed with its share of ballads and musical layering.

However, "Perry Mason", which launches the album with tremendous force, survives as evidence of Ozzy's intentions, along with "Thunder Underground" and "My Jekyll Doesn't Hide", both co-written with Zakk Wylde and Geezer Butler.

"Perry Mason", written by Ozzy, Wylde and John Purdell, carries the combined clout of Wylde's heavy guitar riffing, Geezer's rumbling bass and a synthesizer arrangement, and it immortalizes the famous TV lawyer played by Raymond Burr.

The name came first – Ozzy scribbled it down as a potential title – and the lyrics were written to fit, opening, typically enough, with a murder. "Who can we get on the case?/We need Perry Mason..."

I JUST WANT YOU

"I wrote this song with Jim Vallance in his studio in Canada," said Ozzy. "It was one of those magical days when everything seemed to be working. We sat there and came up with these incredible lines – 'There are no impossible dreams/There are no invisible seams'... And after all those incredible things said in the song, the one line, 'I don't ask much, I just want you,' seemed to be a nice way to sum it all up."

Ozzy was enjoying the experience of working with professional songwriters. He recalled: "I've always worked in a band environment where we just jam through stuff and work things out as we go. Previously, the band would spend the first two hours talking about what they were up to last night, how many chicks they got a blow job off, how many beers they'd drunk, how many titty bars they'd been to... working with real songwriters is a whole learning process for both parties."

He added: "I was first paired with Mark Hudson and Steve Dudas and I was amazed at how quickly it was coming out... I've had a lot of fun with them on the way, too – and while I won't be using all the stuff we wrote, I'll be keeping a good part of it. Then came the Jim Vallance thing. I think Jim and I learned a lot off each other."

"I Just Want You" takes a measured pace, and again features the synth, but a big guitar sound and a thumping rhythm section add enough power. The track became a great favourite through its exposure on MTV.

SEE YOU ON THE OTHER SIDE

Ozzy, Zakk and Lemmy together came up with one of Ozzy's most personal songs about death and the afterlife. Much was made of the fact that this ballad was written after American comedian Sam Kinnison died in a head-on car smash and Steve Marriott, former Small Faces and Humble Pie frontman, was burnt to death in a bedroom fire.

But Ozzy himself explained: "I wrote that song for my wife. I absolutely adore my wife. The love that I have for her and the love she has for me will never die. I truly believe that if I pop off first or she goes, then we'll meet up on the other side. I believe in life after death, which is strange because at one point, I didn't believe in life after birth.

"I believe in life after death because I'm getting closer to it now and I'm at the half-way point at least! It's like a message to Sharon because I love her."

Sharon has been quoted as saying: "Ozzy wrote that song when he was really ill earlier this year and he was being wrongly diagnosed. He was told that he had an illness that was really bad and we thought that that was it, that he was going to die. That's where it came from."

A new poignancy now surrounds the song with the news of Sharon's battle against cancer and Ozzy's worried revelation: "I've done a lot of praying, believe it or not."

This is widely considered to be the best of the album's slow songs with its metal-edged melody and some expressive guitar work from Wylde.

MY LITTLE MAN

Once again choosing a subject close to his heart, Ozzy declares his devotion to his son Jack. Now an unlikely sex symbol through his TV exposure on "The Osbournes", the gawky and accident-prone Jack was almost ten at the time *Ozzmosis* was released.

Opposite: All grown up at last? Ozzy faces his demons, literally and figuratively, as he enters his final phase as a creative musician.

"Don't you know that I love you more than life itself," sings Ozzy, with unashamed pride and tenderness. "I'd like to keep you with me all your life but I know I can't do that."

The blatant sentimentality of the lyrics, coupled with the relatively gentle musical environment, irritated many fans. Others were happy to discover a soft side to Ozzy's personality, and they have pointed to the harnessed power of the band and a cracking Wylde guitar solo as redeeming qualities.

It is also thought that the slow but darker album track "Denial" addresses Ozzy's confused relationship with Jessica, his daughter by first wife Thelma.

"My Little Man" was one of the songs that came from Ozzy's partnership with Steve Vai, who claims that the singer originally planned to use both him and Zakk Wylde on the album but that his contributions were vetoed by the record company.

He told Steven Rosen that in his writing sessions with Ozzy, "we got some great, great stuff." He added, "After I met Ozzy, I really started to like him a lot. He was a lot of fun all the time... He's really a pretty wild guy."

OLD LA TONIGHT

Reportedly written around the time of the LA riots, "Old LA Tonight" is usually interpreted as being a song about home and hearth, bringing the album to a tranquil end with evocative, Rick Wakeman piano, synth and guitar play – a sound which again divided the fans.

While admitting to a vulnerability and uncertainty about the future, the song exhibits a positive element, with a one-day-at-a-time hopefulness about the choruses: "It's gonna be all right in old LA tonight."

Ozzy has been shuttling between LA and England for years with his family, his blunt Brummie wit somehow weathering the Hollywood humour by-pass.

He said: "I love it here, although I don't think I could ever live full-time in the US. The thing about going back to England is that it's quieter and calmer and I can collect myself more easily. As it happens, Malibu is one of my favourite places ever – better than Hawaii, better than anywhere in the States."

He also enthused: "The great thing about LA is that everyone minds their own business. Apart from Sharon not getting on with the neighbours." And another "bonus": "If anyone gets into my house out there, I would have no hesitation in blowing his head off. I've never kept a gun in the house in England, but I will keep one in LA."

"One" would seem a modest tally...

With the *Ozzmosis* album, and tracks like "Old LA Tonight", Ozzy finally showed his hand as a home-loving, family man – at least since he sobered up – as well as a TV addict who loves nothing more than a night in front of the History and Discovery channels.

He said: "I've come to the conclusion that people don't want to know the truth – that I'm a happily married man with three kids that I absolutely adore, and that what I do is entertain people. I am not fucking Dracula."

With "The Osbournes", Ozzy would learn that millions of people finally did want to know the truth.

Other tracks on the album are the mellow and persuasively melodic "Ghost Behind My Eyes", which describes a nightmarish torment; and the haunting "Tomorrow", a moody track punctuated with clamorous choruses, while Ozzy's treated vocals add an effective peculiarity to the mix.

Opposite: Buff, sober and working the programme, Ozzy Osbourne hit the stage at around the turn of the millennium in the best shape of his career.

THE 2000S & BEYOND

SINCE THE START OF A NEW MILLENNIUM, BLACK SABBATH HAVE
REMAINED A HUGELY POPULAR LIVE ACT. IN ADDITION, OZZY BECAME
A REALITY TV STAR, AND TONY IOMMI AND GEEZER BUTLER REUNITED
WITH RONNIE JAMES DIO – THE SINGER'S LAST HURRAH. THEN, IN 2013,
CAME THE FIRST NEW SABBATH ALBUM WITH OZZY IN 35 YEARS.

In the years between 2000 and 2013, the four original members of Black Sabbath experienced the best of times and the worst of times.

In 2000 came a belated recognition of their contribution to music: their first and only Grammy award. They won Best Metal Performance for the version of 'Iron Man' from their 1998 live album *Reunion*, recorded at Birmingham's NEC in December 1997.

Tellingly, the award was for a song that was 30 years old – not for either of the two brand new studio tracks that were included on Reunion. These new songs, 'Selling My Soul' and 'Psycho Man', were underwhelming. The band would again struggle for inspiration when they attempted to make a new album in 2001 with producer Rick Rubin. As Geezer Butler explained to *Classic Rock*: "We had six or seven songs, but Ozzy wasn't really into it. We didn't really have a direction, so we left it."

The Sabbath album was also aborted because Ozzy chose to make another solo album, *Down To Earth*, which was released in October 2001. What followed was, for Ozzy, an even bigger distraction – the launch in 2002 of MTV reality series *The Osbournes*, in which his family's chaotic domestic life was documented in comic detail. "The idea of the TV thing was an extended version of *Cribs*," Ozzy said. "But it just took off in a way that I still to this day do not understand." The series made Ozzy more famous than ever before.

Then, on December 8, 2003, he almost died in a freak accident. While riding a quad bike in the grounds of his Buckinghamshire mansion, he crashed and broke his collarbone, eight ribs and a neck vertebra. As he recalled to *Classic Rock*: "I was only doing four miles an hour – just my fucking luck, that is. I was in a coma for eight days, died twice and came back."

"I WAS IN A COMA FOR EIGHT DAYS, DIED TWICE AND CAME BACK."

Ozzy Osbourne

Ozzy wasn't out of action for long. In 2004, he was back fronting Sabbath at Ozzfest. He did it again the following year. After that, Ozzy again turned to his solo career. After a series of fair-to-middling albums recorded with his long-time guitar cohort Zakk Wylde, in 2010 Ozzy revisited his usual formula of old-duffer-recruits-young-axe-hero by shedding Wylde in favour of Firewind shredder Gus G. As a result, fans expected the new record, *Scream*, to be a guitar-centric album, and while there were a couple of showcases for G's startling soloing ability, the album wasn't as heavy as some might have predicted. In fact, the production by Ozzy veteran Kevin Churko was softer and more poppy than 2007's *Black Rain*, which was dominated by Wylde's riffs.

This often worked just fine, with 'Time' and 'Soul Sucker' turning out to be anthemic power ballads that sales reps could nod their heads to on the freeway, but it was a less successful approach on the more beefy tunes. A large portion of this album ('Fearless' for example) was devoted to dreary fists-aloft shouting rather than the slick melodicism on which Ozzy had been making his name since 1980. There was just too much filler: songs like 'Latimer's Mercy' and 'Crucify' – and the

cringeworthy single 'Let Me Hear You Scream' – made classics like Crazy Train seem as if they were recorded in a parallel universe.

Meanwhile, Iommi and Butler reconciled with Ronnie James Dio and Vinny Appice to record three new songs for the compilation album *Black Sabbath: The Dio Years*. A tour followed, for which they took the name Heaven & Hell – in honour of Dio's greatest work with Sabbath, and because the Sabbath name was retained for the original line-up. In 2009 came a new album, *The Devil You Know* – described by *Metal Hammer* as "a truly awesome achievement". But on May 16, 2010, Ronnie James Dio succumbed to stomach cancer. For Iommi, Butler and Appice, there was at least some small consolation in knowing that Heaven & Hell had provided one final golden era in Dio's brilliant career. "What a great singer he was," Iommi said. "It was just a certain magic that we had with him."

Opposite: And it's goodbye from them; Black Sabbath wound up their live career with a spectacular final tour, calling it The End and taking two years to do it properly.

Above: Geezer Butler, Ozzy Osbourne and Tony Iommi, elder statesmen for whom ill-health and advancing years have called time. But where's Bill Ward?

OZZFEST 2001

THE ORIGINAL BLACK SABBATH

FEATURING

OZZY OSBOURNE   TONY IOMMI   GEEZER BUTLER   BILL WARD

Slipknot

TOOL

PAPA ROACH

AMEN   SOULFLY   DISTURBED

ZAKK WYLDE'S
BLACK LABEL SOCIETY   (hed) PLANET EARTH   RAGING SPEEDHORN   THE UNION UNDERGROUND   APARTMENT 26

Your Host For The Day   KRUSHER

Village Of The Damned   FEATURING: EXOTIC NIPPLE PIERCING, BODY PAINTING,
TATTOO PARLOUR AND THE HOUSE OF HORROR

THE NATIONAL BOWL at MILTON KEYNES
Saturday 26th May 2001 Show Starts:11.00am (subject to licence)

Tickets: £32.50 (including VAT) Available by Credit Card Tel: 0870 602 1143 (24hrs) (subject to booking fee).
Buy online at www.buyupfront.com Priority club members use www.musicmastercard.co.uk

Immediately after Dio's funeral, Iommi spoke again with Ozzy. As Iommi explained: "I was in LA for the funeral, and Ozzy called me. He said he was going back to England in a week and asked if we could get together and have a chat. That's what we did. Ozzy and Sharon came up to my house." Iommi knew that the conversation would lead to the original band reforming. "Ozzy had indicated that to me on the phone," Iommi said. "Of course, Geezer and myself were free to do something at that time."

On November 11, 2011 it was announced that Black Sabbath – Osbourne, Iommi, Butler and Ward – were making a new album. Just two months later, however, Iommi revealed that he had been diagnosed with lymphoma, a form of blood cancer. The prognosis was uncertain, and as Iommi later said: "What frightened me to death was the professor saying, 'It could be a permanent thing or it could go.' I was thinking, oh, fucking hell – great!" Iommi began treatment, and decided that work was the best therapy. Making the album would give him something positive to focus on.

Unfortunately, it was an album that Sabbath would have to make without Bill Ward. On February 2, 2012, Ward issued a statement via Facebook in which he said: "I would love nothing more than to be able to proceed with the Black Sabbath album and tour. However, I am unable to continue unless a 'signable' contract is drawn up." The issue was not resolved, and Bill Ward was out.

Later, when questioned about the contract that had been offered to Ward, Ozzy pleaded ignorance. "I don't know what deal went down," he said. "I don't understand it, I never have, and I don't want to. Just

leave me alone with the fucking music. That's my gig." Ozzy also insisted that there was no bad blood between the two parties. "I'm not putting Bill down," he said. "I love the guy, and I wish him well."

After the final show of The End tour was performed in Birmingham on 4 February 2017, Sabbath went on what appears to be a permanent hiatus. BMG embarked on the Ten Year War reissue campaign, when the Ozzy-era LPs were converted into a new audio format, MQA, and released as a £300 box set and a crucifix-shaped USB stick. Iommi was so involved in the promotion that he came down and did an interview on stage at Sabbath's old Denmark Street studio Regent Sound, surrounded by intoxicated journalists.

Only a couple of months later, Sabbath promoted a DVD of their last show called The End Of The End, a rather tasty bit of product that summed up the band's last few years nicely. But that won't be the end of it. Black Sabbath have come through the New Wave Of British Heavy Metal, hair-metal, thrash metal, nu-metal, emo and metalcore, all of which trends were thought to be serious threats to Sabbath's classic sound – but which ultimately didn't even come close to toppling them from their throne. Drug and booze addiction hasn't stopped them. Dodgy management and record companies couldn't stop them in the 70s and 80s. Even the ultimate adversaries, old age and ill-health, haven't overthrown them yet.

And if you read between the lines of recent interview quotes, it's clear that Sabbath's dominion isn't over quite yet. Ozzy told *Rolling Stone*, "I'm not saying I'll never record with Tony or Geezer again," and Geezer added, "There's nothing stopping us from doing another album after the tour". As for Iommi, the man on whom it all depends, he'll never say never.

So don't say a fond farewell to Ozzy, Iommi, Geezer – and even Bill – just yet. Heavy metal never dies, remember, and nor will Black Sabbath, at least not any time soon.

Opposite: The "original" Black Sabbath of Ozzy Osbourne, Tony Iommi, Geezer Butler and Bill Ward reunited for Ozzfest 2001. The band were supported by Slipknot, Tool and Papa Roach at the Milton Keynes Bowl event.

Below: The four Sabbath founder members, seen here at the Golden Gods awards in Hollywood in 2013, before Bill Ward withdrew due to what he called "an unsignable contract".

(2013)

TONY IOMMI WAS BATTLING CANCER. BILL WARD HAD QUIT. AND YET, IN THE
MOST DIFFICULT OF CIRCUMSTANCES, BLACK SABBATH CREATED AN ALBUM
THAT WAS COMPARABLE TO THEIR GREATEST RECORDS FROM THE EARLY 70S.
"WE WANTED TO DO A GREAT PIECE OF WORK," OZZY SAID. "AND I THINK WE DID."

After Bill Ward left Black Sabbath in February 2012, Tony Iommi, Geezer Butler and Ozzy Osbourne did not at any point think about giving up on the new Sabbath album. As Iommi said: "We'd already waited a bloody year. We all thought, we've just got to get on with it."

Ozzy was equally determined to see this through. "I would have loved to have done the album with Bill," he said. "But we got to this point where we thought: we're all in our sixties now. It's now or never."

By the time that Ward's departure was made public, the bulk of the album was already written. Iommi had been stockpiling material for a number of years. The best of it – dozens of riffs, and a few more fully structured songs – was collected on CDs that he presented to Ozzy and Geezer. They each picked out what they thought were the strongest ideas, and in almost every case, their choices were identical.

Rick Rubin was again enlisted as producer, 11 years after he had worked with the band in their first attempt at making a comeback album. That project had been abandoned at an early stage. Butler explained: "When we played the songs for Rick, we realized that they just weren't very good." In 2012, it was a very different picture. The new songs had the power the vibe of vintage Black Sabbath. One of them, 'End Of The Beginning', was evocative of the song from which the band had taken its name back in 1969.

It was exactly what Rick Rubin wanted to hear. As Butler recalled to *Classic Rock*: "Right at the start, Rick got us all together in the studio and played us the first Sabbath album. He said: 'This is what you were. It's not really metal. It's blues-based, but with these evil riffs.' He wanted us to keep it like that."

This much was simple. More complicated was the process of finding a new drummer. Bill Ward was as important to Black Sabbath as John Bonham had been to Led Zeppelin and Keith Moon was to The Who. Replacing him was no easy task. Ozzy suggested the drummer in his solo band, Tommy Clufetos. Rubin said no, believing that Sabbath required someone of greater experience than Clufetos. To this end, Rubin proposed that they should try Ginger Baker, formerly of Cream. This idea was quickly rejected, for two reasons. While Baker is renowned as one of

rock's most brilliant and innovative drummers, he has a reputation for being extremely difficult. Also, he has frequently expressed a loathing of heavy metal. Not the right man for Black Sabbath.

Rubin had another suggestion – this time, a better one. Brad Wilk was the drummer for two bands that Rubin had produced, Rage Against The Machine and Audioslave. At first, Iommi was unconvinced. He admitted: "When Rick suggested Brad, I don't know that we were all that keen on the idea." But Rubin was persuasive. Wilk had a few informal jam sessions with Sabbath – a nerve-wracking experience for a man who had been a fan of the band since childhood. Iommi liked what he heard from Wilk, an expressive style reminiscent of the drummer in The Jimi Hendrix Experience. "Brad reminded me of Mitch Mitchell," he said. "The same style of playing." Wilk got the job. Finally, the album could be completed.

It was recorded at a studio named Shangri-La, situated in Malibu, California, and owned by Rubin. Even at such an advanced stage, new songs emerged as Iommi developed ideas in the studio. "A couple of tracks were written from scratch," Iommi explained. "Just coming up with a riff there and then." One of these tracks was 'Zeitgeist', a beautiful acoustic piece that Iommi crafted in the image of 'Planet Caravan'. Another was the best song on the entire album, with a phenomenally heavy riff and lyrics by Butler on the subject of religious fanaticism. "I wanted to call that song 'American Jihad'," Butler said. In the end, a slightly less inflammatory title was chosen: 'God Is Dead?'

According to Ozzy, Rick Rubin proved a hard taskmaster. "There were times," he said, "when Rick had me in there singing songs for five hours. He would say, 'Do it again! Do it again! That's great, fabulous, but do it again!' I was like, 'What the fuck, Rick? But you know, he did a great job. We all did."

Finally, after 35 years, there was a new Black Sabbath album with Ozzy Osbourne. Titled *13*, it was released on June 10, 2013. *Rolling Stone* magazine said that the album "revisits, and to an extent recaptures, the crushing, awesomely doomy spectacle of their first few records." It was also a huge success, topping the charts in nine countries, including the US and the UK.

And if this proves to be the final Black Sabbath album, then Ozzy Osbourne will have no regrets. "All I wanted to do for so many years is make another Sabbath album," Ozzy said. "I'm just happy that we've pulled it off – even without Bill. It's a fucking great album. And now that it's done, I'm at peace with myself."

Opposite: EDrummer extraordinaire Tommy Clufetos, who sat in for Bill Ward on the final Sabbath world tour. Brad Wilk of Rage Against The Machine played drums on the last album, *13*.

Above: Ozzy Osbourne, pushíng 65 but still delivering the goods on stage like the professional madman of the Seventies.

ACKNOWLEDGMENTS

With special thanks to Scott McKenzie for research, Stephanie Jones for the 'diversional reading', Diana Perkins for her practical solutions, Ian Gittins and Lorna Russell for the opportunity, Robert Smith for his swashbuckling leadership, Ozzy worldwide webmasters without whom etc etc and Nigel and Eve O'Brien, as ever, for being simply brilliant

CREDITS

The publishers would like to thank the following sources for their kind permission to reproduce the pictures in this book.

Key: t = top, b = bottom, l = left & r = right

Alamy: Everett Collection Inc. **66-67**; /Globe Photos/ZUMAPRESS. com **13b, 24-25**; /Pictorial Press **10**; /Trinity Mirror/Mirror **117**; / Will Vragovic/Tampa Bay Times/ZUMAPRESS.com **159**

Getty Images: Richard E. Aaron/Redferns **2, 44r, 78, 128-129**; /Jorgen Angel/Redferns **59, 65, 83**; /Paul Bergen/Redferns **155**; /Larry Busacca/ WireImage **116b**; /Francesco Castaldo/Archivio Francesco Castaldo/ Mondadori Portfolio **6**; /Fin Costello/Redferns **71, 72t, 73, 89, 93, 95, 96-97, 99, 121**; /Colin Fuller/Redferns **51tl, 51br, 54, 56**; /DMI/The LIFE Picture Collection **136**; /GAB Archive/Redferns **49**; /Ron Galella/WireImage **142**; / Gems/Redferns **61** (bottom); /Martyn Goodacre **143, 144**; /Gijsbert Hanekroot/ Redferns **31, 34-35**; /Larry Hulst/Michael Ochs Archives **84**; /Mick Hutson/ Redferns **7, 110, 145, 146, 147, 150, 152-153, 154**; /Michael Marks/Michael Ochs Archives **70**; /David McGough/DMI/The LIFE Picture Collection **86**; /Robert Knight Archive **137, 141**; /Kevin Mazur/WireImage **158**; /Paul Natkin **45,106-107**; /Kevin Nixon/Guitarist Magazine **29**; /Michael Ochs Archives **11, 13t, 33**; /Jan Persson/Redferns **26**; /Ellen Poppinga - K & K/ Redferns **9t**; /Michael Putland **16, 37, 38, 39, 40, 41, 43, 48, 53, 58, 139**; / Ebet Roberts/Redferns **114-115, 127, 131**; /Peter Still/Redferns **80, 101, 125**; /United News/Popperfoto **133**; /Chris Walter/WireImage **12, 19, 20-21, 30, 32, 111**

Photoshot: LFI **46**

REX/Shutterstock: AP **87**; /Roger Allston/Associated Newspapers **124**; /Andre Csillag **76-77, 85, 92t, 92b, 102-103, 105, 113, 116t**; /Ian Dickson **51r, 57, 64**; /Kevin Estrada **62, 63**; /Kent/Mediapunch **69**; /Andrew Kent/Retna Ltd/Mediapunch **75, 79, 81**; /Bill Kostroun/AP **149**; /Alan Messer **55**; /Ilpo Musto **119, 122-123**; / Startraks **157**; /Geoffrey Swaine **112**; /Dick Wallis **74**; /Bill Zygmant **4**

Tracks Images: **60**

Additional photography: Carlton Books Ltd

Every effort has been made to acknowledge correctly and contact the source and/or copyright holder of each picture and Carlton Books Limited apologises for any unintentional errors or omissions, which will be corrected in future editions of this book.